NOT THEM BUT US
In Praise of
the United Nations

JOHN FERGUSON

Gooday
Publishers

First Published in 1988 by Gooday Publishers
P.O. Box 60, East Wittering, West Sussex PO20 8RA

© John Ferguson 1988

British Library Cataloguing in Publication Data

Ferguson, John, 1921 –
  Not them but us : in praise of the United
Nations
  1. United Nations – History
  I. Title
  341.23'09

ISBN 1 – 870568 – 08 – 7

Typeset in Plantin by Woodfield Graphics, Fontwell, West Sussex.
Printed in Great Britain by Hollen Street Press, Slough Berks.

For
Felicitas Richter
And All Those Who Are Working
In the GDR for Peace
Through the UN

Contents

Foreword

For forty years the twin pillars of my witness for peace have been the Fellowship of Reconciliation, where, as a Christian, I can express my understanding of Christ's way of peace, and the United Nations Association where I can work with non-Christians and with Christians whose understanding of Christ differs from mine, but whose concern for peace is equally real. I am proud to have been (at an interval of more than 25 years!) National Chairman of both bodies. I joined UNA executive when Lord Cecil, Lord Lytton, Lord Perth, Dame Adelaide Livingstone, Dame Kathleen Courtney, Gilbert Murray, Will Arnold-Forster, Freda White, Lady Hall and others of that calibre, were in the lead. An institution which they served can hardly be without very strong things to commend it. This is an expression of thanks to them, and to more recent colleagues and fellow-workers for peace all over the world.

I believe in the UN. Not uncritically. It is what we make it. It is a necessary organ for international co-operation; we should use it more and more effectively. If it were not there we should have to invent it. As Robert Muller has said, if the UN went out of existence, it would lead to World War III. And that would mean humankind going out of existence. Instead we have mutual co-operation in the common interest. We need and can have more.

The book was written before the election of Dr Federico Mayor of Spain as Secretary-General of Unesco, before the publication of the Brundtland Report, before the third Special Session on Disarmament. It seemed better not to alter the text to allude to these and other events.

Once again I am indebted, as so often, to Lesley Roff, for her uncomplaining secretarial skills and to my wife, for her encouragement in so many ways, not least in the practical provision of an index.

John Ferguson

1

1 The UN—What It Is And What It Is Not

The United Nations is not a blueprint for world government. It is not a world state. It is an instrument for the nations, divided as we are, to co-operate with one another—if we choose. It offers a meeting-place.

In the modern world it is not possible to 'go it alone'. We cannot isolate ourselves in an independent cocoon. We have become One World, whether we like it or not. The Black Death knew no frontiers. Nor will the Nuclear Winter, if it should come. We are dependent upon one another, and involved with one another. The First World War began with the assassination of an Austrian archduke at Sarajevo, and before long Germany and Russia and France and Britain, and nearly all of Europe, and much of the rest of the world were dragged in. We need a place to meet, to talk together, to slang one another if we like: Winston Churchill once said that jaw-jaw is better than war-war. The UN provides that forum.

There are those who would like to see the UN becoming something more like a world state. There are proposals, for instance, for a second Assembly, representing not governments but peoples. It is wholly right for those who believe in these things to advocate them with all the fervour at their command. But we are not there yet. At the formation of the UN in 1945 the British government were as firm as any other that they would not tolerate any reduction in national sovereignty beyond that which we accept by being a member of a world organization, contributing to its budget, accepting the structures we ourselves helped to form, and earmarking a portion of our forces for UN work if required (Art. 43).

So the UN is there—imperfect no doubt, but the best agreement we could reach. An American senator reached the age of ninety. He was asked, 'Well, Senator, how do you feel?' He replied, 'Not so bad, when you consider the alternative.' The alternative to the UN is chaos.

People tend to talk about the UN as 'them'. But the UN is not 'them'; it is 'us'. The UN has no existence apart from the nations which compose it. The Secretary-General and his staff are there to fulfil the decisions of the nations, no less and no more. U Thant, the first Asian to hold that office, wrote in his memoirs: 'There is a widespread illusion that the Secretary-General is comparable to the head of a government. He is often criticized for failure to take an action—when over 130 sovereign member states collectively fail to act. The plain fact is that the United Nations and the Secretary-General have none of the attributes of sovereignty and no independent power.' So if you hear anyone saying 'The UN has failed,' say to them, 'I'm glad you admit your failure. Now what are you going to do about it?' We are the UN; its failures are our failures and its successes are our successes.

Margaret Thatcher, writing in *New World* in 1985 to celebrate forty years of the UN, said this:

> The United Nations has achieved more than most people would have thought possible in the dark days of world war. And it is right that its achievements should be judged by those realistic and practical standards rather than by some starry-eyed ideal.
>
> The reality is that the United Nations cannot be effective without the co-operation of individual states. The United Nations is not some kind of super-state. What it can do—and has done—is to encourage civilised standards of international behaviour by member states and to secure the resolution of international disputes by peaceful means.

This is written into the very Charter of the UN. All previous international treaties (which is the status of the UN charter in international law) had begun something like 'We the High Contracting Parties....' But the UN Charter begins uncompromisingly: 'We the peoples. . .' We are the United Nations. Not our governments or our ambassadors, but we, the peoples. Let us never forget it.

It is good to remind ourselves of the Preamble to the Charter, which remains one of the great statements of human co-operation:

> We, the peoples of the United Nations, determined to save succeeding generations from the scourge of war, which twice in our lifetime has brought untold sorrow to mankind and
>
> to re-affirm faith in fundamental human rights, in the dignity and worth of the human person, in the equal rights of men and women and of nations large and small, and
>
> to establish conditions under which justice and respect for the obligations arising from the treaties and other sources of international law can be maintained, and
>
> to promote social progress and better standards of life in larger freedom, and for these ends
>
> to practise tolerance and live together in peace with one another as good neighbours, and
>
> to unite our strength to maintain international peace and security, and to ensure, by the acceptance of principles and the institution of methods, that armed force shall not be used, save in the common interest, and
>
> to employ international machinery for the promotion of economic and social advancement of all peoples have resolved to combine our efforts to accomplish these aims.

Note that the four aims are peace, human rights, respect for international law and fullness of life for all; the four means are living together as good neighbours, uniting our strength to maintain peace and security, ensuring that armed force shall not be used save in the common interest, and the employment of international machinery to secure that fullness of life. It is just to say that the aims are more sharply defined than the means, perhaps inevitably.

The United Nations was born out of the furnace of war. The phrase was first used on 1 January 1942 when 26 nations united in continued resistance to the militaristic dictatorships of Germany, Italy and Japan. The broad nature of the new organization was drawn up by China, UK, USA and USSR in 1944. It was in origin the instrument of the victorious powers. There were originally 51 Member States.

But it did not remain so. The League of Nations had run adrift at least partly because it did not have universality of membership. The USA withdrew; Germany and Russia were too long excluded. And vast areas of the globe were colonial dependencies, and unrepresented except through their imperial rulers.

Not so with the UN. It has achieved virtual universality of membership. Switzerland has somewhat strangely remained outside, though co-operating in the work of some of the Special Agencies. South Africa has been excluded for the time being because of its apartheid policies, which are repugnant to the majority of humankind. But, these apart, to all intents and purposes, all independent states are members of the UN. This in its turn creates problems. Of course it would be easier to attain agreement between, say, the states of Western Europe than between the states of both West and East. Easier, though not easy or palatable, as the record of the European Community reminds us. But a UN without the East or without the West would no longer be an instrument which could contribute significantly to peace between East and West. Of course it would be easier to attain agreement between the states of Black Africa than between the states of both Europe and Africa, North and South. But a UN which did not include both South and North would be valueless for the worldwide promotion of better standards of life in larger freedom.

It is arguable that the greatest achievement of the UN has been the peaceable passage from colonial dependency to political independence on the part of large numbers of nations in Asia, Africa, the Caribbean and the South Pacific, so that there are now almost 160 independent member-states of the UN. Some of them have been through difficult passages: we sometimes forget our own past history of civil war and riot. When all is said, it forms an achievement without parallel in history.

Remember other facts too. We write and stamp a letter and mail it to Australia or the USA or India with just as much confidence that it will arrive as if we were sending it to a town in Britain. This does not happen by chance or magic. It happens because of the agreements reached through the Universal Postal Union (UPU), a Specialized Agency of the UN.

Not long ago I had occasion to visit India. It was shortly after Russia's reprobation for her adventure in Afghanistan. It was the more of a surprise to be told that we were flying over Kabul, having been over the Soviet Union for several hours. It is through the International Civil Aviation Organization (ICAO), a Specialized Agency of the UN, that we have the right to overfly other countries and to land at their airports, and it is the ICAO which insists on the highest standards of safety and security at all international airports. On the return journey from that same conference we were about to take off from Delhi when the airport was closed by fog. We were delayed beyond the time when the fog had cleared because international regulations now required the pilots to get adequate sleep before taking the plane on to Karachi. In one sense it was infuriating; in another it was comforting to know that, because of the UN, our lives were not at the mercy of weariness.

We watch the weather charts on TV and take the insights of the weather-forecasters for granted as they move the clouds and sunrays across the map. But without the exchange of weather information through the World Meteorological Organization (WMO), a Specialized Agency of the UN, they would be reduced (as in a famous George Morrow cartoon) to watching the cat in the Meteorological Office wash its face.

In these, and countless other ways, which we seldom realize, the UN is constantly with us to our lasting benefit.

2 A Little History Of International Co-operation

There were visionaries in the ancient world, practical visionaries too. Among the warring city-states of ancient Greece there were a few, like Isocrates, who pleaded for the unity at least of the Greek world. They thought perhaps that they might best find that unity in facing a common enemy—Persia. And when they had unity imposed on them by the imperial power of Macedon, a brilliant militarist, Alexander the Great, did indeed lead the forces of the Greeks to conquer Persia and to sweep far into central Asia, to Tashkent and Samarkand, and down into India. On his return to Mesopotamia he tried to establish a partnership in rule between Greeks and Persians, and though his proud Macedonians jibbed, he won them over for the moment. For even if Alexander did not, as one historian (W. W. Tarn) maintained, have a vision of the Unity of Mankind, he did seek a wider unity than the Greek world offered.

Alexander died, tragically young, and his empire fell apart, though never back into the old small units. Federal constitutions were now in the air, and there were all kinds of experiments. But above all the barriers were broken and the horizons had receded. Plato thanked the gods that he was born a Greek and not a 'barbarian', but Diogenes, nicknamed 'the Dog', threw off all such local attachments and declared 'I am a citizen of the universe,' and the philosophers of the new age, Stoics and Epicureans alike, declared that there was in nature only one people, mankind, and one country, the earth, and that political divisions were artificial.

Rome came, and took over the Greek world as well as Western Europe and North Africa, in the process giving to a larger area of the globe a longer period of untroubled peace than at any time in the history of humanity *either before or since*, an astonishing and

7

rather frightening fact. The Romans were ruthless conquerors, and in their early days vicious exploiters of the conquered. But they came to see the virtues of assimilation, and gradually came to grant Roman citizenship, first to meritorious individuals, then to communities, till by AD 212 virtually every citizen of any community in the Empire was also a citizen of Rome. Further, though Rome conquered by military might, she ruled by consent. The whole of North Africa from the borders of Egypt to the Atlantic was policed by a single legion based on Lambaesis in present-day Algeria, nominally 6,000 men but always under strength. Despite frontier wars many legionaries must have been engaged in public works rather than military action, which explains why the Christian Church could tell converted soldiers or conscripted Christians not to contract out, but not to take life. The Roman secret seems to have been to encourage the universal loyalty and the genuinely local or municipal loyalty but to break down the intermediate loyalties which might (like our modern nationalisms) be destructively divisive. It was as if a person were a citizen of Chichester and the United Nations, but not of Sussex, England, UK or the European Community. Roman powers of assimilation were remarkable. Even in the first century BC Roman culture was being revivified by people from the area we call North Italy, but they called 'Gaul our side of the Alps', such as Catullus or Vergil. In the first century AD we find leading writers and statesmen coming from Spain. A century or so later they were looking to North Africa. The next century saw emperors from Syria and the Balkans, and by the fourth century AD Gaul was the leading centre of Roman civilization. Europe never wholly lost its memories of Rome as a centre of unity: witness the so-called Holy Roman Empire, which Voltaire declared to be neither Holy nor Roman, though it was certainly an empire.

Meantime a small people, the Jews, whose religious insight has had an effect on history far beyond their own numbers, had its own visions, of swords beaten into ploughshares, and spears into pruninghooks. The Hebrew concept of peace, *shalom*, extends far beyond the absence of war: its root meaning of wholeness encompasses the whole idea of well-being and fulfilment, and still reminds us that there is no peace as long as there remain human beings who are hungry and are not fed, who are oppressed and are not liberated. Among them appeared Jesus, who stood in the line of the Hebrew prophets, and proclaimed fresh values to a troubled world: 'Blessed are the peacemakers.' His words to one of his followers who tried to defend him by violence, 'Put your sword into its place. All those who take the sword shall perish by the sword,' were taken for two and a half centuries to be an authoritative statement of the escalation of violence, and the necessity to renounce it. At the same time his followers saw him as breaking down the barriers which divided Jew from non-Jew or Gentile, and creating a new community in which differences of race, class and sex were irrelevant. This was the Christian Church, and though it has been far from fulfilling the way shown by its founder, it has been potentially a major instrument for peace. (In Asia Buddhism has carried a similar potential, with its commitment to the refusal to take life, and its deep compassion, though Buddhists, like Christians, have a sorry record of violence.)

In Europe, after the break-up of the Roman Empire, the Christian Church was the main factor making for unity and drawing together the warring kingdoms and principalities and dukedoms. The clergy were stringently forbidden to take part in bloodshed (though in 1182 with a curious literalism the Archbishop of Mainz fought in battle with a mace rather than a sword to avoid shedding blood). Even the laity had to do penance for lives taken: the Normans after the battle of Hastings had to do forty days' penance every year for each Saxon life they took.

This did not prevent Europe being racked with wars. In the tenth century, the Archbishop of Bordeaux tried to limit the destruction by initiating the Peace of God, exempting from violence specified non-combatants, clergy, women, unarmed peasants and merchants. In the following century the Truce of God tried to add further limitations. In general there was to be no fighting from Thursday to Sunday each week in honour of Christ's sufferings, none at all during Advent and Christmas, Lent and the period from Easter to Pentecost. It should be remembered too that the Crusades, however deplorable episode in other ways, were a serious attempt to achieve peace in Europe by international organization directed to an external enemy and for a common purpose of bringing the Holy Places of Palestine into Christian hands.

A further feature of this period was the development of a Christian doctrine of the Just War, which went back to Cicero, and was brought into Christian thought by Ambrose and Augustine. About 1140 Gratian in a major document began to shape international law by defining conditions in which war might be properly called just. Gratian was an important pioneer. His work, sometimes imprecise, was sharpened by his followers Rufinus and Huguccio, by Hostiensis in the thirteenth century, by the monumental genius of Thomas Aquinas, and by some of the great theologians of the sixteenth century.

Meantime, Islam had unified a vast area of the world from the Atlantic to India, and showed remarkable tolerance towards Jews and Christians in the process. The *umma* or brotherhood of Islam was like 'a single hand, like a compact wall whose bricks support each other'. The essential view of the Qur'an is of a single worldwide community: one God, one mankind, one law, one ruler. Wars were carefully analysed into those which are wars of disobedience and unjustified, and those which are wars of obedience and justified. The halting of Muslim expansion meant that the world was not a single theocratic state; it was divided between *dar-al-Islam*, the territory of Islam, and *dar-al-harb*, the territory of war. Within the brotherhood of Islam, war was strictly outlawed. Arbitration was encouraged within Islam, and permitted between Muslim and non-Muslim communities. Outside, war was strictly controlled: for example, unbelievers must be given a chance to accede to Islam before fighting began; it was not permitted to kill enemies in flight; non-combatants were to be spared, and (according to some) domestic animals also.

In Europe in 1517 Erasmus wrote *The Complaint of Peace* in which he claimed to speak for Peace herself. 'In all countries the greater part of the people certainly detest war and desire peace.' So in the following centuries emerged schemes of world order. In 1595 (published much later) came the Grand Design of Henri Quatre. He proposed a parliament of Europe representing six hereditary monarchies (France, England, Spain, Sweden, Denmark, Lombardy), five elective monarchies (the Papacy, Holy Roman Empire, Poland, Bohemia, Hungary), four republics (Venice, Italy, Netherlands, Switzerland). There were also to be a senate and half a dozen minor councils.

In 1623 Emeric Crucé extended this idea in *The New Cyneas*. The importance of this work is twofold. First, he looked beyond Europe and included China and the Indies. Second, he held that wars were caused by clashes of economic interest, and advocated free trade and commercial co-operation.

In 1625 Hugo Grotius, horrified at the war-wasted condition of Europe, wrote his famous work on the rights or laws of war and peace, aiming to replace war by law, and violence by arbitration.

Several years later the Quaker William Penn published his essay *Towards the Present and Future Peace of Europe*. He proposed a Parliament of Europe with weighted representation. Austria was to have 12 representatives, France and Spain 10 each, Italy 8, England 6 and so on—'and if the Turks and Muscovites are taken in, as seems but fit and just, they will make ten apiece more.' It is interesting that Penn, writing as a Christian, does not confine his Parliament to Christians. He expounded seven benefits of his scheme: the prevention of the spilling of so much human and Christian blood; the recovery in some degree of the reputation of Christianity; the money that would be saved; the destruction that would be avoided; the ease and security of travel and trade; the security against the Turks; the increasing degree of friendship between the nations.

In 1712 the Abbé de St. Pierre put forward his immensely influential *Project for Perpetual Peace*. It was based on *The Grand Design of Henri Quatre* and proposed a perpetual union of European monarchs, with a chamber of commerce, and a senate of 24 deputies (one from each state) in a City of Peace. The most important new proposal was for common action against any monarch who defied the Senate.

Fifty years later Jean-Jacques Rousseau gave his own mellifluous version of St. Pierre, with a permanent congress, of which he had worked out the details including quotas of payment.

11

He too insisted on common action against any who break the agreed statutes, and a guarantee of territorial integrity. Rousseau foresaw the need for changes, and thought that after five years they might be made on a simple majority vote, and thereafter on what we loosely call a 'two-thirds majority' (meaning that a proposal should receive two-thirds of the votes of those present and voting).

Jeremy Bentham, the English Utilitarian philosopher, in 1786 made proposals of characteristic common sense. Bentham's most important proposal was for an international tribunal basing its decisions at any time upon the greatest good of the greatest number: this dream eventually found fulfilment in the International Court of Justice. He proposed a Congress of the Nations, realizing that it would not easily enforce its decisions, but (equally realistically) recognizing that public opinion can itself be an effective force. He was well ahead of his time in looking to the limitation and control of armaments, and to the independency of colonial territories.

In 1795 an even greater philosopher, Immanuel Kant, took up the theme in his book *Towards Perpetual Peace*. He proposed a Federation of Free States with republican constitutions. There were to be no secret treaty clauses (a century and more later Woodrow Wilson insisted on 'open covenants of peace openly arrived at'), no annexations, no standing armies, no violent interference in the affairs of another state, and no national debt contracted in foreign affairs. If war should break out, it was to be conducted under strict rules and limitations. He proposed 'conditions of universal hospitality', meaning freedom of travel and welcome to travellers. He held the optimistic view that 'the commercial spirit ultimately controls every state and will compel world peace.'

The Napoleonic Wars put an end to such grandiose schemes in Europe, though we should not forget that similar ideas sustained the remarkable experiment of the United States of America, which has not merely held in federal unity (one civil war apart) up to fifty states with their own legislatures, but has shown an extraordinary facility for assimilating people from all over the world so that, for better or worse, they become distinctively American.

In the nineteenth and early twentieth centuries, arbitration was a recognized mode of international action in cases of dispute. From 1820-40 there were eight such disputes, from 1841-60 there were 30, from 1861-80 there were 44, and from 1881-1900 actually 90. During the American Civil War a ship called the *Alabama* sailed from Liverpool, and served as a privateer in the interests of the South. After the war was over the US government claimed damages from Britain. The matter went to arbitration in 1872 and judgement was given against Britain and a fine imposed of £3,000,000, a large sum in those days. Gladstone, as Chancellor the Exchequer, paid the fine in despite of public opinion. In 1880 he looked back on the episode and said: 'We regard the fine imposed on this country as dust in the balance compared with the moral example set when these two great nations, England and America, which are among the most fierce and most jealous in the world with regard to anything that touches national honour, went in peace and concord before a judicial tribunal to dispose of painful differences rather than have recourse to the arbitrament of the sword.' Again in 1902 there was a boundary dispute between Chile and Argentina. King Edward VII of Britain was called to be arbitrator. He gave his decision, the line was established, and on the new line running through the high mountains of the Andes was placed a great statue of Christ with an inscription which proclaims that never again should these two nations war with one another; nor have they.

A little-known episode towards the end of last century concerns a Quaker bearing the illustrious name of Fox. He felt a call to tell the Tsar of Russia that war was wrong. Most people would have shrugged it off as an idle fancy, but Fox was tenacious. He went to Russia and secured an appointment with the Tsar. The Archbishop was present, but Fox said, 'I wish to see you alone, sire,' and the Archbishop was, to his fury, dismissed. 'What do you want with me, Mr. Fox?' 'I have come to you, sire, with a message from Almighty God.' ' I am always delighted to receive a message from the Almighty. What does he bid you tell me?' 'He bids me tell you, sire, that war is wrong.' 'Indeed, Mr. Fox. That is a very interesting assertion. Would you explain it?' Fox expounded the Quaker witness to peace. The Tsar asked some

13

shrewd questions and, when half an hour had passed, said, 'I am very grateful to you, Mr. Fox, for coming to me like this. If I keep you longer, I shall be getting into trouble. Good-day, Mr. Fox.' So Fox came home, and heard no more. Except that some months later came the Tsar's initiative in calling the first Hague Peace Conference, and attempt to secure agreed disarmament and international co-operation. It failed but it was a noble attempt, and anticipated much that was fulfilled later.

The theory of peace at the turn of the century was based on the Balance of Power. This meant simply and crudely that, if the major powers were approximately equally armed, no-one would disturb the peace because the outcome would be uncertain. Today, if a politician speaks of the balance of power, he—or she—almost invariably is advocating an imbalance of power: 'we' must be stronger than 'the others'. This was buttressed by a system of secret alliances so that no-one was certain who was coming in on which side. This theory was blown sky-high at Sarajevo in 1914. We can say if we like that, in a situation of high armaments, a seemingly trivial incident—the assassination of an arch-duke—sets a match to a trail of gunpowder. Or we can say that the danger of such a theory is that a side scenting a temporary tilting of the balance may incline to take advantage of it. Either way, the theory did not work, and there is no reason to suppose that it will do so again. We seem incapable of learning from the past. Charles Beard once said that the only lesson to be learned from history is that no-one ever learns lessons from history.

Out of the ashes emerged that marvellous experiment, the League of Nations. The principle, which emerged out of the war itself, was that of the armed coercion of a law-breaking state by common action. This principle, slightly simplified, meant that if fifty states agree to act co-operatively, and they are all lightly armed, no-one will break the peace, knowing that they will be outnumbered 49 to 1 and they will be reduced with the minimum of bloodshed if they do. This is collective security.

This fell apart on four grounds. First, the League did not have universal membership. The USA withdrew and never joined. The USSR was for a long time excluded. So were Germany and the defeated countries. Secondly, as is sometimes

14

forgotten, the League had a unanimity rule; not merely five great powers but every state had a veto. Thirdly, after the initial disarmament consequent on the end of the war, the victorious powers never disarmed. Philip Noel-Baker used to say that it was clear by 1931 that either Britain and France must disarm to the level of Germany, or Germany would rearm to the level of Britain and France and beyond. We refused the former, and the latter happened. Fourthly, the Great Powers were not prepared to be involved in collective security until their interests were directly involved. By then it was too late. When Japan invaded Manchuria, the British Foreign Secretary (Sir John Simon) was congratulated by the Japanese Ambassador for putting the case for Japan better than he could have put it himself.

A further handicap lay in Woodrow Wilson's attempt to get rid of secret diplomacy by 'open covenants of peace openly arrived at'. It was admirable in theory. But it did not prevent secret diplomacy, and it did hamper agreement. For in international agreements there have to be concessions, and few politicians like making them in public where they may be regarded as acts of weakness. Statements made in public are too often propaganda either for the world or for the home market. The problem has been accentuated in recent years with the growth of TV and instant media coverage. A curious consequence has developed in the UN Security Council, whereby the Council retires to an inner room to seek agreement, and afterwards emerges for a public debate. It is unwise to scorn this as play-acting. A good deal of what is most useful in politics is play-acting.

But all was not loss in the League. It must be recalled that nothing like it had ever been essayed before. It was, said Cecil, a great experiment. One success was the development of the conference, with the Assembly meeting every year and the Council four times a year at least. The habit of conferring offered an alternative to armed conflict, and it should be remembered that as a regular practice it was something new.

Another boon was the development of an international Civil Service in the Secretariat under the guidance of Sir Eric Drummond (later Lord Perth), with a quite extraordinary dedication to peace and capacity to rise above the national origins of the members.

A great stride was made towards the establishment of International Law with the Permanent Court of International Justice. This gave a permanent institution in place of the old *ad hoc* arbitrators. True, its jurisdiction was not compulsory, and of course could not be unless the Great Powers were willing to accept it. The Optional Clause (36) of the Court's Statute allowed voluntary accession to compulsory jurisdiction. Smaller countries adhered; it was their protection against arbitrary action by larger ones.

An attempt was made in the 1924 Protocol to agree to abolish war, with compulsory arbitration, and prompt coercive action on recalcitrant states. It is interesting that Germany and Hungary, France and Czecho-Slovakia welcomed the Protocol, sad that Britain rejected it, partly refusing to forego our own 'right of war', partly not being willing to accept international decisions with which we might disagree.

Coercion did not necessarily mean war. Economic sanctions could also be applied, and this was the decision over Italy after her aggression against Abyssinia (Ethiopia). There is little doubt that the oil embargo would have been effective had it been rigorous, but it was not. Again there is a weakness in the unwillingness of nations to sacrifice their own economic interests for the common good. This can be seen in relation to South Africa in recent years. More remarkable was the episode of the USSR's ill-fated incursion into Afghanistan. The Carter administration in the USA cut off grain-supplies, the Reagan administration, though more hostile to the USSR, restored them under pressure from Mid-West farmers.

The League had its political successes. The invasion of Albania by the Yugoslavs in 1922 was promptly stopped, and evacuation took place within nine days. The war between Poland and Lithuania was ended. The invasion of Bulgaria by Greece came to an instant halt and reparations were made. There were other examples. They showed what could be done.

Alongside the political structures were the astonishing work of the International Labour Organization under its inspired Director-General, Albert Thomas, who was instrumental, through

16

a series of detailed conventions, in getting countries to legislate for improved industrial conditions; the recommendations of a succession of Economic Conferences; action in a wide variety of areas, such as concern for the resettlement of refugees (indelibly associated with the name of the explorer Nansen), the White Slave Traffic, the Drug Traffic, the Protection of Minorities; the Committee for Intellectual Co-operation (the precursor of UNESCO), which was trying to get internationalism established as a basic human idea, and which achieved a great deal within its own limits.

Again and again it has to be recalled that nothing like this had ever been tried before.

The League failed to keep the peace. It is arguable that the means were there, and that we did not use them, and as a result were plunged into disaster again.

Out of the ashes of the League emerged the United Nations, like some phoenix. It too was in origin an organization of the victorious allies. But these included the USA and the USSR. The unanimity rule, which under the League applied to every member, was now limited to the five great powers, as they then seemed, USA, USSR, China, France, UK. This was, and remains, realistic for two reasons. First, without such a protection none of these five would have entered the organization, and none would remain within it. Second, it is an acknowledgement that none of those five can be coerced without a world conflagration. The formal structures of the UN offer no solution to global conflict between the two Great Powers. But the UN offers many possibilities of informal contact, the habit and practice of co-operation and detente, indirect pressures from the rest of the community.

Like the League, the UN espoused collective security. But the nuclear bombs dropped on Hiroshima and Nagasaki made this a dead letter almost before it was formulated. With the immense destructive powers of modern weaponry there is no collective security in military action, only collective insecurity. It is doubtful if the nations have really come to terms with this in working out the alternatives in terms of good offices, more effective jurisdiction, economic sanctions, and other possibilities, though peace-keeping has been an exciting new enterprise.

The purposes of the UN stand as follows:

To maintain international peace and security;

To develop friendly relations among nations;

To co-operate internationally in solving international economic, social, cultural and humanitarian problems and in promoting respect for human rights and fundamental freedoms;

To be a centre for harmonizing the actions of nations in attaining these common ends.

The structure of the United Nations is not so very different from that of the League. It has six main organs: the General Assembly, the Security Council, the Economic and Social Council, the Trusteeship Council, the International Court of Justice, and the Secretariat. All, except the International Court (in the Hague) are located in New York at the UN Headquarters, the diplomatic crossroads of the world. But members of the wider UN family of organizations are located all over the world.

The General Assembly, the nearest approach to a parliament of mankind, meets each year from September to December, with the right to call special or emergency sessions. It is the main deliberative body of the UN, but its resolutions are recommendations only. The Security Council alone has the authority to initiate action. But under the famous 'Uniting for Peace' resolution the Assembly can act upon a threat to peace if the Security Council is paralysed by a veto. On any major issue, a two-thirds majority is required.

The Security Council is charged with executive action, and in particular with the maintenance of peace and security. It has 15 members (enlarged from its original number with the growth of the UN), five permanent (China, France, UK, USA, USSR) and the rest elected by the Assembly for a term of two years. Decisions, which are binding on all Members (an extraordinary waiving of national sovereignty), require nine votes; these should strictly include the affirmative votes of the five permanent members, but it has been valuably established that abstention does not constitute a veto.

The Economic and Social Council had no parallel in the League. It accounts for a major portion of the active work of the UN, work that is seldom heralded in the media. It co-ordinates the work of the specialized agencies such as World Health Organization (WHO), Food and Agriculture Organization (FAO), United Nations Educational, Scientific and Cultural Organization (UNESCO), International Labour Organization (ILO), International Atomic Energy Agency (IAEA), International Telecommunications Union (ITU), International Civil Aviation Organization (ICAO), World Meteorological Organization (WMO), General Agreement on Tariffs and Trade (GATT), World Intellectual Property Organization (WIPO), Universal Postal Union (UPU), Inter-Governmental Maritime Consultative Organization (IMCO), International Fund for Agricultural Development (IFAD). Then there are the four financial agencies located in Washington, DC, including the World Bank and the International Monetary Fund (IMF), the five programmes financed by voluntary contributions, the UN Development Programme (UNDP), the World Food Programme (WFP), the UN Children's Fund (UNICEF), the UN Relief and Works Agency for Palestine Refugees in the Near East (UNRWA) and the UN Fund for Population Activities (UNFPA), and the Regional Commissions in Africa, Asia and the Pacific, Europe, Latin America, and Western Asia. It must be few of the general public who realize just how much the UN is doing.

The Trusteeship Council was established to ensure that Governments responsible for administration of Trust Territories took adequate steps to prepare them for self-government or independence, and magnificently they have done their work. Ten of the eleven Trust territories have been brought to independence (Namibia is in a separate category, and has its own Council).

The International Court of Justice exists for the peaceful settlement of disputes voluntarily submitted to it, and to give advisory opinions on questions of international law. No state is required to submit to its jurisdiction, but if it does it is bound to comply.

The Secretariat, headed by the Secretary-General, provides the international civil service. Its members, drawn from nearly 140 nations, are bound by oath not to seek or receive instructions from any Government or outside authority. To date there have been five Secretary-Generals, Trygve Lie from Norway, Dag Hammarskjold from Sweden, U Thant from Burma, Kurt Waldheim from Austria, Javier Perez de Cuellar from Mexico. Each has made a distinctive contribution.

Though the structures resemble those of the League, the United Nations is in many ways a great advance on the League. Its membership is more nearly universal; its instruments for encouraging economic and social co-operation immeasurably wider. And, as we have seen, it is rooted in the concept of 'We, the peoples'.

3   The Settlement Of Disputes

When the average person thinks of the record of the UN in the peaceful settlement of disputes, arguably its primary function, their minds probably focus on the conflicts in the Near East, and the Gulf, or on the Indian subcontinent, or in Cyprus, in which, though the presence of the UN has greatly reduced and checked the incidence of violence, no permanent solution has been reached. Or they may think of unhappy examples of Great Power involvement, in Korea or Vietnam, Tibet, Hungary or Afghanistan, or even the Falkland Islands. They seldom look at those situations of tension which, because of the UN, have not reached the stage of open conflict. It is reckoned that over forty years the UN has been faced with nearly 200 conflicts, the majority of which have been resolved without war.

It is important, of course, to note that the UN is under certain proper limitations as to its spheres of action—proper, in the sense that they are constitutionally agreed, and though there are those who find them unduly restrictive, no major power would agree on their withdrawal.

The first is that the UN may not intervene in the domestic affairs of its States-Members. This is Article 2 (7) of the Charter: 'Nothing contained in the present Charter shall authorize the UN to intervene in matters which are essentially within the domestic jurisdiction of any state or shall require the Members to submit such matters to settlement under the present Charter, but this principle shall not prejudice the application of enforcement measures under Chapter VII.' Thus the UN had no jurisdiction in the civil war in Nigeria or in the Sudan. Nigeria might have welcomed a UN presence, but to invite it would have been to admit Biafran independence. Similarly, and almost more sensitively, the UN has no jurisdiction in the conflict in

Northern Ireland, and to invite a UN peacekeeping force (in many ways preferable to the presence of the British Army, which is inevitably seen as *parti pris*) would be to admit beforehand that the Republic of Ireland has a legitimate interest in the North. It is true that the UN may intervene if there is outside interference with an independent nation (though it is more difficult when the outside presence is invited by the accepted government), and has a proper concern that the conflict shall not spread to neighbouring states. It is true too, that the passing of the Universal Declaration of Human Rights through the Assembly on 10 December 1948 (now Human Rights Day) meant that the nations accepted in some sense a responsibility for the preservation of those values in other countries, and their own liability before the world for their maintenance of human rights. The principle remains.

Secondly, the executive power in the UN rests with the Security Council, and, as already explained, the assumption was that if the five Great Powers were divided, improvident action might accelerate world war. There are two modifications to the unanimity rule. By case law abstention from voting is not deemed to break unanimity, and so does not inhibit action. And a party to a dispute has no vote. In the present form Article 27 (3) reads: 'Decisions of the Security Council on all other' (i.e. non-procedural) 'matters shall be made by affirmative vote of nine members including the concurring votes of the permanent members; provided that, in decisions under Chapter VI, and under paragraph 3 of Article 332, a party to a dispute shall abstain from voting.'

The third qualification is that a state under attack has the right of self-defence. In the world as it is, this is an obviously necessary regulation. But it leads to situations where a country may legitimately bypass the UN to the detriment of the UN's standing. Under international law Britain was justified in going to the military assistance of the Falkland Islands after they had been subjected by aggression from Argentina, an aggression unanimously condemned in the Security Council. But suppose that, instead, Britain had asked the Security Council to act. They would almost certainly have applied mandatory economic sanctions to Argentina, which according to economists, would have brought down the Argentinian government within six months and ended the occupation. There would have been no loss of life. The lesson for Argentina and other potential aggressors would have been not 'Don't take on someone bigger than yourself,' but 'Don't offend against international law'. There would have been a better chance of a lasting solution, and the standing of the UN and of International Law would have been enhanced. The British action was neither illegal nor improper, but a chance was missed.

But with these caveats now look at some UN actions.

During the war Russian troops were stationed in N. Iran to secure the trade-routes. On 19 January 1946, Iran complained to the Security Council that the Russians were intervening in their domestic affairs. The Security Council brought delicate pressure to bear and Russian troops were completely withdrawn by May.

In the same year, French and British troops were thought to be lingering unduly long in Syria and the Lebanon. The matter was raised in the Security Council, and a somewhat bland resolution was vetoed by USSR. Britain and France got the message, and, though there was no formal resolution, the troops were all withdrawn by the end of the year.

On 30 July 1947, Australia and India drew the Security Council's attention to fighting between Indonesia and the Netherlands. The Security Council pressed for a ceasefire and appointed a three-member Good Offices Committee, which was instrumental in achieving the Renville Agreements in January 1948. Eleven months later the Dutch repudiated these Agreements and reopened military operations. The Security Council called for a ceasefire and the return of political prisoners, and this was achieved. On 28 January 1949 the Council recommended a federal independent state with a transfer of sovereignty and democratic elections. The Good Offices Committee became the UN Commission for Indonesia and was responsible for restoring peace, and bringing the two sides together in a Round Table Conference. Dutch troops were evacuated in the presence of UN military observers. Indonesia became independent on 27 December 1949 and the UN Commission spent a further year and a half in observing the implementation of the Hague agreements.

In two instances in 1948, the Security Council was asked to consider states in the Indian subcontinent, Junagadh and Hyderabad. In both cases the UN decided rightly not to intervene. In the first a plebiscite indicated a preference for accession to India rather than independence or accession to Pakistan; in the second the Nizam withdrew a request for assistance.

In Greece, UN involvement discouraged encroachment by Greece's neighbours and helped to preserve Greek territorial integrity. It was also responsible for securing the repatriation of Greek children who had been taken to Yugoslavia.

In the early 1950s, in the face of failure in agreement between France, UK, USA and USSR, the General Assembly secured the independent statehood of Libya and Eritrea.

At much the same time, a number of controversial and dangerous issues came before various organs of the UN. These included tension between USA and China, between Britain and Iran, between Yugoslavia and USSR, between Burma and Taiwan. In all these, although there were no formal UN decisions, the discussion helped a peaceable resolution of the conflict.

Korea was another matter. This was a curious episode. The USA and USSR had established a joint commission to set up a Provisional Korean Democratic Government. There was no agreement, and the USA took the matter to the General Assembly, who set up a special commission. The USA withdrew its forces under observation; the USSR claimed to have done the same. The UN Commission informed the Secretary-General on 25 June 1950 of aggression by North Korea. It happened that the USSR were boycotting the Security Council at the time, and were not present to interpose a veto. Collective military action was therefore taken, and sixteen nations participated. This checked the incursions but failed to produce a unified Korea, and protracted armistice negotiations did no more than establish a demarcation line and demilitarized area.

On 20 December 1952, the General Assembly called for a Peace Treaty for Austria. Action was slow, but on 15 May 1955 the Austrian State Treaty was signed, and on 14 December Austria joined the UN.

24

In 1956 Russian troops intervened in Hungary. The Hungarian Government insisted that this was a domestic matter, but on 2 November asked the Security Council to arrange for the withdrawal of Russian troops. This was vetoed by the USSR. The General Assembly then voted for Russian withdrawal, access by UN observers, and free elections, but the Hungarians were unco-operative. However the Secretary-General established a fact-finding committee and for five years maintained his own Special Representative. Four important things followed from UN concern. First, the International Red Cross Committee organized relief on behalf of the UN. Second, the UN High Commissioner for Refugees co-ordinated work for refugees. Third, world concern prevented the situation from deteriorating further. Fourth, across the subsequent thirty years Hungary has been at peace, and by a process of quiet change has achieved an order which combines some of the virtues of Eastern Europe with some of those of Western Europe.

In the second half of the 1950s, open discussion in the UN eased tensions between Syria and Turkey, Sudan and Egypt, USA and USSR, Saudi Arabia and Britain, and in the early 1960s, between Dominican Republic and Venezuela, Italy and Austria, USA and Cuba, Kuwait and Iraq, Cambodia and Thailand, Yemen, UAR and Saudi Arabia, Haiti and Dominican Republic, Malaysia and UK, Panama and USA, Malaysia and Indonesia, India and Pakistan. It is not of course suggested that the UN provided lasting solutions in these disputes, but it is clear that, without the UN, any one of them might have produced a major conflagration.

One of the most dangerous episodes of this period was the so-called Cuban Missiles Crisis. Two features of this are sometimes forgotten. First, all three of USA, Cuba and USSR appealed to the Security Council. Second, it was the Secretary-General who made a personal appeal to Kennedy and Khruschev to suspend arms shipments and negotiate, and to Castro to suspend installation. Subsequently he paid a personal visit to Cuba to see the situation for himself. On 7 January 1963 he received a joint letter of appreciation from USA and USSR, a thing which can rarely if ever have happened.

There were more disputes aired and eased in the second half of the 1970s, between Zaire and Portugal, Guinea and the Ivory Coast, Spain and Morocco, Haiti and its neighbours, Equatorial Guinea and Spain, Zambia and Portugal, Britain and Iran, Guyana and Venezuela, Senegal and Portugal. A number of these dealt with alleged Portuguese violations of independent African states. Constant assertions by the Security Council that the independence of these states must be honoured, and pressures of world public opinion, had their effect.

A particular example of the Secretary-General's good offices was over the securing of the release of passengers and crew from hijacked planes: an El Al plane hijacked to Algiers, and a TWA plane hijacked to Damascus.

The Nigerian civil war provides a good example of what the UN can and cannot do. A civil war is in the strict sense an internal matter and does not come within the jurisdiction of the UN. The Secretary-General explored the possibility of using his good offices for peacemaking, and decided rightly that this would be most effectively done through the Organization for African Unity (OAU). In addition with the agreement of the Nigerian government, the Secretary-General appointed his personal representative for humanitarian purposes, and he, with the co-operation of UNICEF, the World Food Programme and the International Red Cross, was able to provide relief which saved thousands of lives. Again, special observers were able to accompany the Nigerian forces and check their behaviour.

Now let us for a moment look at precisely what the nations have undertaken under the UN Charter.

All Member States have subscribed to the following:

Article 2 (3) All members shall settle their international disputes by peaceful means in such a manner that international peace and security, and justice, are not endangered.

(4) All members shall refrain in their international relations from the threat or use of force against the territorial integrity or political independence of any state, or in any other manner inconsistent with the purposes of the United Nations.

33 (1) The parties to any dispute, the continuance of which is likely to endanger the maintenance of international peace and security, shall, first of all, seek a solution by negotiation, enquiry, mediation,

conciliation, arbitration, judicial settlement, resort to regional agencies or arrangements, or other peaceful means of their own choice.

Just over a century ago, in 1880, W. E. Hall wrote, 'International law has no alternative but to accept war, independently of the justice of its origin, as a relation which the parties to it may set up, if they choose, and to busy itself only in regulating the effect of the relation...hence both parties to every war are regarded as being in an identical legal position, and consequently as being possessed of equal rights.' This is no longer true. International law does not accept war. We need reminding of our obligations.

Further, under Article 33 of the Charter, we have found identified the main forms of peaceful settlement—negotiation, enquiry, mediation, conciliation, arbitration, judicial arrangements and resort to regional agencies or arrangements. Keith Suter of Australia, in a valuable discussion in *Alternative to War*, enlarges on these. Good Offices, mediation and conciliation make use of third parties. They are variant forms of a common technique, appealing to commonly accepted standards. International arbitration and international courts call for a third party to give judgement.

Peaceful settlement of disputes involves an emphasis on peace, but not peace at any price, or peace that papers over cracks, but the resolution of deep-seated issues so that they do not endanger international security. Peaceful settlement of disputes almost always involves a third party, a mediator or arbitrator. Peaceful settlement of disputes is not confined to a single method.

We must distinguish between peacemaking, peacekeeping and peacebuilding. Peacemaking is a legal and political process aimed at achieving a negotiated settlement. Peacekeeping uses military or paramilitary forces in a non-military way to keep enemies apart. Peacebuilding is the political, economic and social task of removing the causes of conflict, both general and particular, including the task of fostering disarmament, and the task of giving to peace a positive content.

The regional arrangements referred to above are spelt out in Chapter VIII of the Charter, which encourages local co-operation on large or small scales, and explicitly says in Article 52 (2) that states entering into such arrangements 'shall make every effort to achieve pacific settlement of local disputes through such regional arrangements and by such regional agencies before referring them to the Security Council'. This is common sense. It prevents them becoming the play of Great-Power politics. It places responsibility where there is greatest understanding. It leaves a further point of reference. These systems have had their successes in Africa and in the Americas in particular.

Keith Suter writes: 'Two concluding points—both of amazement—should be made. It is amazing that there should now be any international conflicts at all when the network of peaceful mechanism which now exists is recalled. On the one hand, there are up to three levels through which nations have to go before resorting to war. On the other hand, at each level there are various forms of peaceful settlement machinery available to them. It is also amazing that this wide range of forms of peaceful settlement machinery should receive so little publicity. In legal terms, the preparation of such machinery is a growth industry. In political and publicity terms, it is virtually unknown.'

It is indeed amazing. Once again we are confronted with the fact that the UN provides us with the means to peace. It is we who fail to use them. Where we do use them, the successes have been notable.

4   Peace-Keeping

One of the most exciting developments in the United Nations has been the development of a totally new technique of peace-keeping which was not even foreseen at the founding of the UN at Lake Success. Secretary-General Javier Perez de Cuellar spoke of this at length in Helsinki in April 1983, and said, 'Peace-keeping is widely and rightly regarded as one of the most successful innovations of the United Nations in the years since the Charter was signed.'

He pointed out that the peacekeeping forces, the soldiers in blue helmets, are nothing to do with the concept of a United Nations force being formed to repel aggression, though they are in fact recruited under Article 43 of the Charter by which states-members agree to earmark a portion of their armed forces when called on by the UN. Those recruited are members of the armed forces, precisely because that is the undertaking, and because there is, by and large, no other standing group on whom the members can immediately call in an emergency, though the Scandinavian countries have tended to use their reservists, and, in the special circumstances of the Congo, Nigeria provided police as well as soldiers. It would be an interesting concept if one of the more liberal-minded nations recruited a standby group of conscientious objectors to normal military service for this sort of operation.

Each operation has its own individual mandate, terms of reference, and conditions of work. The troops are always stationed with the consent of the country or countries concerned. They are placed in an area of conflict or potential conflict, and their purpose is to discourage recourse to violence while a solution to the cause of conflict is pursued by diplomatic means. They are not empowered to resolve the conflict, but to prevent it from spreading.

They are equipped with light arms only. They are in international law permitted to use them only in self-defence or in defence of positions they have been authorized to occupy. Even in these instances, they in fact lose credibility if they have recourse to arms, as happened in the Congo, when they were attacked by mercenaries. They are in essence a non-violent force in a violent situation. Their task is to avoid adding to the sum of violence. They are not empowered to intervene militarily if fighting breaks out between the two parties to the conflict. They lack—deliberately—the equipment or numbers to stop a major military action by military counter-action. They are the voice of conscience, which was once cynically defined as the uncomfortable feeling that someone may be looking. They are the instrument of world public opinion.

The Secretary-General rightly began his account of the development of peace-keeping with the use of observers. This device was first used by the UN Special Commission on the Balkans in 1947. They were investigating the situation in Northern Greece and allegations that the civil war was being fostered by Greece's northern neighbours. The Commission was largely formed of professional diplomats who found that they lacked the expertise to evaluate a military situation. So they co-opted their military attachés from the embassies in Athens, and were able to obtain a much more objective and accurate assessment, which in turn meant that the extent of infiltration across the frontiers decreased, and with it the danger that the war might become an international conflict.

This operation was so successful that two official missions consisting of military observers were established in the following two years. One was set up in Palestine to check the maintenance of the truce achieved in the 1948 war, a rôle which it carried out effectively. The other was in Kashmir to monitor the cease-fire between Pakistan and India, and to avert frontier violations. This group had astonishing success. It comprised no more than fifty observers covering a long and controverted frontier. Yet their presence was sufficient to avert fighting over a period of some twenty years, with the sole exception of a breach during the 1965 war, a conflict which had nothing to do with Kashmir in its inception.

Another remarkable operation at much the same time took place in West Irian. Here the issue was decolonization. There was need for an independent administration during the period of transition from Dutch colonial government. A caretaker administration was formed by a multi-national team of only thirty-five experts appointed by the UN, and met with remarkable success in achieving a peaceful handover.

The first example of a peacekeeping force in the stricter sense came in 1956 after the British and French débacle over Suez. Action in the Security Council was vetoed by Britain and France. The Assembly called for peace. On 7 November a UN Peace-Keeping force was agreed. On 12 November it arrived, more swiftly than a second-class, and sometimes a first-class, letter takes to travel from one town to another in Britain. It must be recalled that the operation was without precedent. The force consisted of troops from Brazil, Canada, Colombia, Finland, India, Indonesia, Sweden, Yugoslavia and (most remarkably) a joint contingent from Denmark and Norway. The troops were organized in their own national contingents, both because of language problems and because of differences of military practice. This made the Denmark-Norway unit the more exceptional and commendable in breaking down the barriers.

Israel were unco-operative. The UN troops could operate only on the Egyptian side of the frontier. This, and the continuing hostility, made their achievement all the more remarkable. They kept the peace for eleven years. For eleven years there was a chance to keep it cool. For eleven years the peace-makers had a free hand. That they failed in the end was no discredit to the peacekeeping force; it was due to the intransigence of the situation, and to the ambitions and military optimism of Nasser. Further, peace in the Gaza strip led to relative prosperity on both sides of the frontier, for Israel as well as Egypt, and enabled the Red Sea to be reopened to shipping.

31

The troops were withdrawn in 1967 on Nasser's orders. UN forces may not infringe the sovereign rights of member-states; they cannot enter or remain without the invitation of the government in whose territory they are stationed, and properly so. U Thant, Secretary-General at the time, pleaded earnestly with Nasser to allow the troops to remain, and was brusquely rejected. This act of Nasser's underlines his responsibility for what happened. It is a sobering thought that, had they not been withdrawn, there would have been no more conflict on that frontier. As it is, they demonstrated, as a pilot scheme, something of what could be done; they provided a notable example of international co-operation; and, as we have noticed, at least gave the inhabitants of that troubled region a decade of peace and prosperity.

In the Congo, the future Zaire, the Belgians withdrew on 30 June 1960 leaving a country notably ill-prepared for independence; the absence of trained indigenous personnel is a serious indictment of the Belgian colonial régime, and actually called some commentators to speculate whether their withdrawal was not deliberately premature in the hope that they would have to be recalled to produce order from the ensuing chaos. The chaos certainly ensued. On 11 July an appeal was made to the UN, on 13 July the Security Council met, on 15 July the first troops arrived from Tunisia and Ghana. The speed of action is astonishing. The troops were there for four years. Their achievement is clear. They restored law and order, they saved the country from external intervention, they maintained its territorial integrity, they saved it from civil war, they protected human rights. Two features marked off this operation from the one in the Gaza strip. The UN forces, as already noticed, were engaged in fighting, when they were attacked by mercenaries who were active in the Congo. They did not seek the fighting, and in international law they had the right of self-defence. Also the UN intervention covered a far wider span of concern than in any of the other operations. They were involved in policing the country; the Nigerians sent trained police, but the soldiers had to do police work also; this went beyond the normal rôle. They were also involved in political and technical assistance. There is

32

no problem about the latter, but there is proper uneasiness about the UN becoming involved in a nation's internal politics.

Further use of observers in the Yemen followed in 1963-4. Then in 1964 came the third opportunity for the peacekeeping force. This was, and is continuing, in Cyprus. The civil strife which tore Cyprus apart was exacerbated by the involvement of Greece and Turkey. For five years there was scarcely a single day on which there was no threat to the peace. The UN force never exceeded 7,000. Yet during that whole period there were only two serious outbreaks of communal violence, and the UN troops never fired even one shot. There were two especially dramatic episodes. In 1966 at Melousha, the UN troops stood between an advancing Greek army and a Turkish village, and said, literally, 'Over our dead bodies.' The Greeks fell back and the situation was saved. At Paphos in 1967, there had been a succession of communal murders. The UN forces began by establishing free and safe movement in the area, and were able to go on from there to hold community meetings. The problems of Cyprus have not been resolved. It can not be too strongly said that it is not the function of the peacekeeping forces to solve problems. All they can do is to check the blood-letting and offer a breathing-space in which solutions may be sought. Both of these have been achieved in Cyprus.

It is perfectly proper within the UN structures for regional organizations to operate in the interests of peace. A good example of this in peace-making was the successful intervention of the Organization of African Unity and the All-Africa Church Conference to bring to an end the protracted fighting in the Sudan. In peace-keeping, in 1965 the Dominican Republic received a regional peace force from the Organization of American States. It was not an ideal operation, since the action, like the Organization, was too dominated by the USA. But it is another example of what can be done.

Leaving out a few instances where observers have been used, we come to the Lebanon. UNIFIL, the UN peacekeeping force, was established in 1978; soldiers from 13 countries have shared in its work. Its mandate was explicit. It had to supervise the withdrawal of Israeli soldiers who were at that time in the

Lebanon. This was successfully and peaceably carried out. It was also charged with controlling the movement of armed personnel within a specified area of the Lebanon, ensuring peaceful conditions in that area, and facilitating the restoration of the Lebanese Government's authority. The UN forces have at no time been charged with ensuring peace throughout the country; their writ never extended to Beirut until after the 1982 Israeli attack when 50 military observers were stationed there. Within the area with which they were entrusted, they were remarkably successful in seeing that peace was maintained, order observed, and prosperity restored. Unfortunately, however, the Israeli government did not allow them access to that small part of their assigned territory directly bordering Israel. They ensured that within their area no weapons were placed capable of reaching Israeli territory. They had no writ to control what happened elsewhere in the country. Nor had they any power to resist the new Israeli invasion; this was in any case not within their mandate; they were not equipped for heavy fighting. They have fulfilled their mandate with courage and tenacity, despite the loss of 89 lives. They have largely prevented infiltration through the area they control. 'They have brought humanitarian assistance to the inhabitants of the area and a higher degree of personal security than is present in the neighbouring communities,' says the Secretary-General with justifiable pride. It is a shame that, in other parts of the Lebanon, some of the Great Powers decided to act for themselves instead of extending the UN mandate. They were not successful, and it was a serious undermining of UN authority.

In January 1985 there were five different UN peacekeeping operations in existence.

A. **Peacekeeping forces**, composed of contingents of armed troops made available by Member States. To recapitulate, these forces assist in preventing the recurrence of fighting, restoring and maintaining law and order, and promoting a return to normal conditions. To this end, peacekeeping forces are authorized as necessary to use negotiations, persuasion, observation and fact-finding. They run patrols and intervene physically between the opposing parties. Peacekeeping forces are armed but are permitted to use their weapons only in self-defence.

1. United Nations Peace-Keeping Force in Cyprus (UNFICYP). This was created in March 1964 under Security Council resolution 186 (1964) to prevent a recurrence of fighting between the Greek Cypriot and Turkish Cypriot communities and to contribute to the maintenance of law and order in the island. It supervises the cease-fire lines and provides security for the civilians of both communities. In December 1984 there were 2,311 troops from Austria, Canada, Denmark, Finland, Ireland, Sweden and UK, under Maj.-Gen. Gunther-Greindl (Austria), and 36 civilian police from Australia and Sweden.

2. United Nations Disengagement Observer Force (UNDOF). This was created in May 1974 under Security Council resolution 350 (1974) to supervise the implementation of a buffer zone between Israel and Syria, in which it has been almost entirely successful. In November 1984 there were 1,306 troops from Austria, Canada, Finland and Poland under Maj.-Gen. Carl-Gustav Stahl (Sweden).

3. United Nations Interim Force in Lebanon (UNIFIL). This was created in March 1978 under Security Council resolution 425 (1978) to confirm the withdrawal of Israeli forces, restore international peace and security, and assist the Goverment of Lebanon in ensuring the return of its effective authority in the area. In October 1984 there were 5,683 troops from Fiji, France, Finland, Ghana, Ireland, Italy, Netherlands, Norway, Senegal and Sweden, under Lt.-Gen. William Gallaghan (Ireland). Subsequently Senegal withdrew, and Nepal offered a replacement.

B. **Military Observer Missions**, composed of unarmed officers made available, at the Secretary-General's request, by Member States. An observer mission's function is to observe and report to the Secretary-General, for transmission to the Security Council, on the maintenance of a cease-fire, to investigate violations and to do what it can to improve the situation.

35

1. United Nations Truce Supervision Organization (UNTSO). This was established as long ago as June 1948 to supervise the truce in Palestine, and subsequently to assist all states in fulfilling the armistice agreements. The Observers co-operate closely with UNDOF and UNIFIL. There are observer group stations in the area of Beirut, and another in Egypt. The authorized strength of UNTSO is 298 from Argentina, Australia, Austria, Belgium, Canada, Chile, Denmark, Finland, France, Ireland, Italy, Netherlands, New Zealand, Norway, Sweden, USA, USSR. The Chief of Staff is Lt.-Gen. Emmanuel Erskine (Ghana).

2. United Nations Military Observer Group in India and Pakistan (UNMOGIP). In 1948 the UN Commission for India and Pakistan was authorized to establish observers as required. The terms of reference of these have changed across the years. At present they supervise a Line of Control agreed by India and Pakistan in July 1972, though they operate only on the Indian side of the line. There are just over 40 observers from Australia, Belgium, Chile, Denmark, Finland, Italy, Norway, Sweden and Uruguay. The Chief Military Observer is Brig.-Gen. Thor Johnson (Norway).

Peacekeeping forces are not a panacea. They are limited by the will of the receiving country and the mandate from the Security Council. Their task is a limited one. They must not be judged for what they are not. The lesson of UNIFIL is not that peacekeeping forces are a failure; if that were so, they would not have been invited by the Lebanese Government to extend their operation for a further period. The lesson is that we need to strengthen the peacemaking function of the UN; and to consider far more urgently what steps the international community can properly take against a nation which refuses to co-operate or which flouts the authority of the UN. But the very list of the nations involved in each operation shows that this is a highly successful piece of international co-operation.

5 Disarmament And Arms Control

The existence of great armaments endangers the peace. Arising from insecurity, it adds to that insecurity. Looking back on the events which led up to the First World War, Lord Grey said, 'The moral of these events is clear. It is that great armaments lead inevitably to war.' The existence of an uneasy and unstable peace in Europe since 1945 does not negate that. As long as the weapons of destruction continue to pile up, the direction is away from peace.

Apart from the insecurity, the dangers arising from accident or error are staggering. The fact that the West was put on nuclear alert 3,854 times between January 1979 and June 1980 must cause alarm; we may assume a similar figure for the East (*International Herald Tribune*). We know of an occasion when the early-warning system at Fort Collins gave notice of a full-scale nuclear attack. The commanding officer refused to act on it, rightly: it was occasioned by a radar echo from the moon. But what is the use of an early-warning system if you do not act on it? And what if he had acted on it? (*Boston Traveler* 13 December 1960). On another occasion a man put a training tape on a computer that was for real. The counter-offensive was ready. The fail-safe time was twenty minutes. Seven minutes thirteen seconds had passed before the mistake was discovered and rectified (*Observer* 2 March 1980). We do not have sufficient sympathy with those who carry the future of the world in their hands, yet have nothing to do day by day. It is not surprising that some turn to drink or drugs or become psychologically unstable. Great care is taken about this; yet we know of some whose request to be taken off nuclear assignments has been refused (L. J. Dumas in *Bulletin of Atomic Scientists* 1980). We are at the mercy of machines which go wrong and human beings who are subject to error,

37

and however great our precautions they can never be 100% secure or anywhere near it.

Recently we have become more clearly aware of the consequence of any significantly large succession of nuclear explosions in the urban areas of the Northern Hemisphere. This is the 'nuclear winter'. A curious variety of scientific investigations came together to enable these conclusions to be reached—from the extinction of the dinosaurs to the records provided by Venus probes. The basic fact would be a huge pall of blackness enveloping the Northern Hemisphere, and spreading far into the Southern, lasting for months. The result would be to exclude the light and heat of the sun. Temperature would plummet below zero; standing water would freeze to a depth of six feet. More, because of the exclusion of sunlight, there would be no chlorophyl. Plants would die, and all creatures which live off plants would die, and this in turn would leave carnivores without food. There would be some hardy insect life; that is all. In addition, the ozone layer, which lies above us as a beneficent protective covering, would be shattered, admitting ultraviolet light in injurious quantities. And this takes no account of the deaths from blast or from radioactive fall-out. The investigation was carried out by a team of scientists, including Russian, British and American. Their conclusions were initially challenged by the Pentagon, who set up their own investigating team, who differed in detail but agreed with the independent investigation on the broad picture.

So arms control and disarmament have been prominent among the concerns of the UN. Article 26 charges the Security Council with formulating plans for the establishment of a system for the regulation of armaments. Article 11 empowers the Assembly to consider the principles governing disarmament and the regulation of armaments. Disarmament is in the very Charter.

Has anything been achieved? Not as much as we could wish. Once again we have to remind ourselves that the UN 'isn't them; it's us.' The UN cannot do more than we are willing to do.

Yet achievements there are. Let us first remember that there are binding pre-war agreements. In particular, the 1925 Geneva Protocol on the use in war of asphyxiating, poisonous and other gases, and of bacteriological warfare, remains in force. Britain, China, France, USA and USSR are all parties to it in relation to all the other signatories. There have been numerous accessions to it since the war, mainly of former non-self-governing territories.

The first major relevant agreement through the UN was the Convention for the Prevention and Punishment of the Crime of Genocide, adopted by the Assembly in 1948. This was followed in 1949 by the Geneva Convention Relative to the Protection of Civilian Persons in Time of War.

In 1952 the Assembly established the UN Disarmament Commission with a limited membership to prepare proposals for the regulation, limitation and reduction of armed forces and armaments, and for the elimination of weapons of mass destruction. This was expanded in 1959 to include all UN members. It failed in its primary object, but up till 1965 was an important forum for expressing concerns about disarmament and ideas for its achievement.

From the mid-1950s also the UN Scientific Committee on the Effects of Atomic Radiation has been assembling, studying and disseminating information on observed levels of ionizing radiation and radioactivity in the environment and on the effects of such radiation upon man and his environment, a vital activity, and one which ought to be more widely publicized. The membership of UNSCEAR comprises: Argentina, Australia, Belgium, Brazil, Canada, Czechoslovakia, Egypt, France, FRG, India, Indonesia, Japan, Mexico, Peru, Poland, Sudan, Sweden, UK, USA, USSR.

In 1959 came an important breakthrough. The Antarctic Treaty created the first nuclear-free zone, and indeed a totally demilitarized zone, covering the whole area south of 60° South. Without the treaty the uninhabited wastes would have been tempting for nuclear tests, and there might have been danger to world peace from conflicting territorial claims. The treaty protects the environment, and resources which should be the heritage of the whole of mankind. More, it is a positive assertion of peace. It provides an example which might be followed in relation to other parts of the world.

In 1963 the Partial Test Ban Treaty banned nuclear explosions (whether for peaceful purposes or military tests) in the atmosphere, outer space or under water, or in any environment where radioactive debris might spread outside a country's own territory. The original signatories, UK, USA, USSR, declared that their purpose was to end contamination of the environment, slow down the nuclear arms race, provide a stage towards a Comprehensive Test Ban Treaty and eventual disarmament. Many other countries have subsequently acceded to the Treaty, including India (who subsequently tested a weapon underground), and Israel, but not, unfortunately, China or France, who have not observed its provisions. The signatories have observed its provisions scrupulously, as they have kept the bilateral USA-USSR agreement limiting the size of any underground tests.

The year 1967 saw two important treaties. The first, the Outer Space Treaty, is important for the principles governing peaceful activities of states in outer space. It is less important for its military limitations. True, it agrees to ban the placing in orbit round the earth any objects carrying weapons of mass destruction, or the stationing of them in outer space; it also forbids the use of celestial bodies for any military purpose. But it does not forbid the entry of ballistic missiles into outer space with a view to re-entry. Hence Star Wars and all that.

Of greater importance is the Treaty of Tlatelolco, which prohibits the testing, use, manufacture, production or acquisition by any means, as well as the receipt, storage, installation, deployment and any form of possession of nuclear weapons in Latin America. The establishment of an inhabited nuclear-weapon-free zone was a logical development of the Antarctic Treaty, and is of the highest importance both in itself and as an example to follow. But there are limitations within the Treaty: Cuba has not signed, and Brazil does not regard herself as bound by the Treaty till all relevant states have signed. Further, nuclear explosions for peaceful purposes are not banned, and this is a distinction not easily made. There remain thus some anxieties about Argentina and Brazil.

Most important of all is the Non-Proliferation Treaty of 1968, widely subscribed to, but not by states who hope to achieve the potential for nuclear weapons. It might be said that this means that the Treaty is valueless. On the contrary it shows its value.

The leaders of the nations take it seriously. By signing they are bound to adhere to it.

The UN named the 1970s as the Disarmament Decade. The achievements were limited but real. They include the 1971 Sea-Bed Treaty, banning from the sea-bed beyond coastal areas all nuclear weapons and installations (though it does not preclude the use of submarines).

In 1972 came the Biological Weapons Convention, prohibiting and preventing the development, production, stockpiling, acquisition or retention of the agents, toxins, weapons, equipment and means of delivery relating to microbial or other biological agents of types and in quantities that have no justification for prophylactic, protective or other peaceful purposes. (The clause must have been drafted by a poet.)

Next, 1975 saw the Helsinki Conference on Security and Co-operation in Europe. The Final Act incorporated a major document on confidence-building measures and certain aspects of security and disarmament. The states agreed the need to eliminate the causes of tension, to strengthen peace and security, to strengthen confidence, to refrain from threats of force, and to reduce the dangers of armed conflict. They therefore encouraged the voluntary prior notification of major military manoeuvres in order to avoid misunderstanding, together with the exchange of observers. There is not much that is binding here. But it is a solemn declaration of intent, and the whole spirit of Helsinki is something on which to build.

In 1977 came the Environment Modification Convention, forbidding any military or hostile use of techniques for modifying the environment. This both eliminates widespread, longlasting and serious damage to the ecology and prohibits the deliberate production of earthquakes, cyclones and the like for military purposes. It is important to realize that, like many of the other conventions, such a convention has an importance in itself, limited but real, and at the same time offers a jumping-off point for a more radical agreement, *if the nations are willing*.

In many ways the most exciting event of the 1970s was the 1978 Special Session of the General Assembly on Disarmament. This was brought about by the non-aligned states and

41

the Non-Governmental Organizations (NGOs), many of whom made significant contributions during the actual session, and who were understandably dissatisfied with the lack of progress towards disarmament. The meeting lasted from May 28 to July 1, and the final document was passed unanimously by all the participating countries except Albania (Brazil and France expressed minor reservations).

The final document is of remarkable quality. It states unconditionally, 'Mankind today is confronted with an unprecedented threat of self-extinction arising from the massive and competitive accumulation of the most destructive weapons ever produced,' and again, 'Removing the threat of a world war—a nuclear war—is the most acute and urgent task of the present day. Mankind is confronted with a choice: we must halt the arms race and proceed to disarmament or face annihilation.' The nations then went on—unanimously it must be remembered—to declare the goal of general and complete disarmament. They placed a high priority on nuclear disarmament and nuclear non-proliferation. They supported measures of limited scope, regional arrangements, the development of nuclear-weapon-free zones, non-proliferation, limitation of the arms trade, reduction of military budgets, confidence-building measures. But they recognized that such steps had not achieved disarmament so far, and that they must be seen as pointing the way to comprehensive measures and to general and complete disarmament.

An important feature of the debate, and of the agreed document, was the recognition that the major political and economic problems of the world are interconnected. Links were made between disarmament, security, good relations between states and the peaceful settlement of disputes, and between disarmament and development in the Third World. The French actually proposed a percentage cut in arms expenditure, the money saved to go to a development fund, but this was not accepted. President Eisenhower once said, 'Every gun that is made, every warship launched, every rocket fired, signifies, in a final sense, a theft from those who hunger and are not fed, from those who are cold and are not clothed.' As an official UN report put it, a billion people can neither read nor write. The cost of two strategic bombers, $200,000,000, would enable UNESCO to solve this problem altogether. Malaria, trachoma, leprosy and yaws could be wiped out through WHO for the cost of one aircraft carrier.

A further factor of importance was that the final document recognized the need to involve the general public in disarmament. It was too important a matter to be left to governments! It stressed that the NGOs had a major part to play in public education on disarmament issues, and urged closer co-operation between the NGOs and the UN.

To agree such an unanimous statement was a remarkable achievement. But apart from the reactivation of the Commission on Disarmament, the strengthening of the Conference on Disarmament to include all five nuclear-weapon states, the establishment of the Advisory Board to provide expert studies, and the strengthening of the UN Disarmament Centre, nothing happened. It did not happen because the most heavily armed powers were not willing for anything to happen. Yet they agreed to the final document.

A Second Special Session was held in 1982. There was considerable international tension at the time and accord was not easy to come by. Nonetheless, (largely through the Swede Inga Thorsson) the nations reaffirmed the final document of 1978, which is thus the official policy of both the Labour and Conservative administrations in this country and of both the Democratic and Republican administrations in the USA, as well as the USSR, China, France. It is for the people of the world to see that their governments fulfil their professions.

The Second Special Session also unanimously launched the UN World Disarmament Campaign, whose aim is to inform, to educate, and to generate public understanding and support for the objectives of the UN in the field of arms limitation and disarmament. Certainly no praise can be too high for the factual and careful analyses they provide.

The tragedy is that the facts are well known and agreed. The practical consequences are well known and agreed. The machinery is available. James McCloy of the US and Valerian Zorin of the USSR together laid down the processes of disarmament if there was the will to disarm. And we know, as Philip Noel-Baker used to say, that the only security for the USA lies in a disarmed USSR, the only security for the USSR lies in a disarmed USA, and the only security for the world lies in both disarming.

Immediate and partial measures are possible. A freeze or moratorium does nothing of itself, but it does prevent escalation from getting out of hand, and at the present levels of overkill it really does not matter if there is theoretically a strategic superiority with one 'side' ('What in the name of God,' asked Henry Kissinger, 'is strategic superiority? What is the significance of it politically, militarily at these levels of numbers? What do you do with it?'—*Foreign Policy* 1974 – 5). Nuclear-weapon-free zones can be developed, as one is being developed in the South Pacific. Why not in the Indian Ocean? In Africa? In Central Europe? East Germans would like a nuclear-weapon-free demilitarized zone in Central Europe: this would give no military advantage to any—how could it? A Comprehensive Test-Ban Treaty is greatly to be desired: Margaret Thatcher has spoken out for it. (Speech at Harrogate 27 March 1982). The loopholes in the Non-Proliferation Treaty must be closed. The negotiations for a Chemical Weapons Treaty must be pressed to a conclusion. These are not enough, but they are valuable of themselves, and could lead to a change of direction.

All these the UN has opened up and made possible. It is through the UN that we have made the statements affirming the need for general and complete disarmament. It is through the UN that we must fulfil our words. The failures and frustrations are not due to the United Nations but to the disunited nations—that's us!

6 The International Court of Justice

The International Court of Justice is a compromise. In saying this we must recognize two things. First, willingness for any such institution to exist is relatively recent. Even arbitration was rare before the nineteenth century. In the nineteenth century, as we have seen, arbitration steadily increased. This led to the establishment of the Permanent Court of Arbitration in 1899, and, eight years later, a careful delimitation of its function and elaboration of its rules. In the years preceding the First World War, the Permanent Court of Arbitration played an important part in settling disputes between states, though it is not at all certain that any of those disputes submitted to it would have led to open warfare. By 1907 there was an increasing sense of the need for a Permanent Court of International Justice. But this was not established till 1920. It has been in existence for no more than two thirds of a century, and in its present form for only forty years.

Secondly, it is a compromise and a necessary compromise. Federalists reasonably say that we shall not have world peace in a full and real sense until there is a system of binding supranational law. This is no doubt true. But until states are willing to give up more of their sovereignty, we have to be content with something less, and it is a basic principle of international law that no state can be compelled to submit to the jurisdiction of an international tribunal without its consent, though if one party fails to appear, the other may call upon the Court to decide in favour of its claim, provided that the Court is satisfied that the claim is well-founded in fact and law, and though, once a state has agreed to its jurisdiction, the verdict is binding. Non-compliance is rare. Since the Second World War and the establishment of the present World Court, there have been two examples only, both involving Britain. In the Corfu Channel case, Albania refused to comply with the judgement, and in the Anglo-Iranian Oil Company case, in which the Court decided it had no jurisdiction, Iran refused to comply with an interim order to preserve the status quo until the issue was resolved. In the event of non-compliance there is resort to the Security Council, though it has never been taken. There is, obviously, a major problem about enforcement procedures. Further, the Court has explicitly no jurisdiction over individuals, on which most systems of law depend. The International Military Tribunal of Nuremberg did not act under international law as validated by the World Court. An individual with a grievance against a foreign country must first seek redress in the courts of that country, and, if that fails, persuade his own country to make it a matter of international justice. There is no cardinal reason why the World Court should not exercise jurisdiction over individuals. The explanation lies 'in the jealous regard of States for their own independence and unfettered sovereignty'. The United Nations can do only what its constituent members are willing for.

Is the Court then valueless? By no means. The very constitution of its judiciary is an achievement. Generally no state is willing for its voice to be unheard in an international body. All member states of the UN, together with one or two others (such as Switzerland), are statutory parties, but it would be patently impracticable to have judges from each, and the judges are limited to 15, one from each of the five permanent members of the Security Council (*de facto* however not *de jure*) and ten more representing 'the main forms of civilisation and the principal legal systems of the world'. No country may have more than one judge. Judges make a solemn declaration that they will discharge their office 'honourably, faithfully, impartially and conscientiously'. Despite this, it is also ruled that the President shall not exercise his functions as President in a case concerning the country of his nationality. It is also ruled that a country party to a dispute may have an *ad hoc* judge on the court, if they are not already represented among the judges. The judges give their verdict by a simple majority vote, and there is no veto. Minority opinions may however be put on record.

Part of the functions of the Court is to give advisory opinions. Requests may be submitted by organs of the UN and by its Specialized Agencies. These advisory opinions are not binding, and the Charter provides no remedy for their non-acceptance, though there is usually no question of this. But occasionally advisory opinions may have strong political implications, and once or twice where they bore on disputes between states the advisory jurisdiction has been successfully resisted. Three notable instances of advisory jurisdiction show the dangers. The first, the Reparation for Injuries case, concluded that where an agent of the UN suffers injury or death in the course of performing duties on behalf of the UN, the UN is entitled to bring action against the state or states responsible for such an injury or death. The immediate application of the general principle lay in the assassination of Count Bernadotte on Israeli territory. Israel was declared legally responsible for reparation, and loyally accepted the judgement; it is hard to know what would have happened had they not done so. The second advisory opinion dealt with the admission of new members—nine states were vetoed by the USSR; five failed to win the necessary majority in the Security Council. The General Assembly asked if it could admit a state which was refused admission by the Security Council. The answer, by 12 votes to 2, was that it could not. The other contentious advisory opinion was over the International Status of South West Africa (now Namibia). The Court held that the obligations of South Africa remained as they had done under the original mandate from the League. South Africa has not complied with this judgement, and, as it was an advisory judgement, there is no direct remedy.

The jurisdiction of the Court includes all cases which the parties refer to it, and all matters referred to its jurisdiction by virtue of the United Nations Charter or in treaties or conventions in force. In settling disputes, the Court applies:

(a) international conventions;
(b) international custom as evidence of a general practice accept-
    ed as law;
(c) the general principles of law recognized by nations;
and secondarily,

(d) judicial decisions and the teachings of the most highly qualified experts of various nations.
(e) the equitable decision *ex aequo et bono* ('according to what is fair and good') if both parties so agree.

Major decisions have related to territorial disputes, as the Right of Passage over Indian Territory (Portugal-India 1960) or the Temple of Preah Vihear (Cambodia-Thailand 1962) or the Maritime Boundary (Canada-US 1981); the Law of the Sea, such as the Corfu Channel (UK-Albania 1949), Fisheries (UK-Norway 1951), the North Sea Continental Shelf (Denmark-Netherlands-FRG 1969), Fisheries (UK-FRG-Iceland 1974); Treaty Interpretation and Diplomatic Protection, such as Asylum (Colombia-Peru 1950, 1951), Rights of US Nationals in Morocco (France-US 1952), Nottebohm (Liechtenstein-Guatemala 1955), Barcelona Traction, Light and Power Company Ltd. (Belgium-Spain 1970), Iran hostages (US-Iran 1979).

A closer examination of one or two of these cases will be helpful. The Court strictly adheres to the principle that no questions but those actually submitted for determination can form the basis of a decision. It comments on no matters except those immediately before it. It passes no judgement, directly or indirectly, on the actions of states which are not parties to the proceedings. These are severe limitations. Equally, it would be exceedingly dangerous if they were not there.

In the Colombia-Peru asylum case Señor Haya de la Torre sought asylum in the Colombia Embassy at Lima. The Court was asked whether Colombia were entitled to identify the alleged offence committed by Haya de la Torre as political without the agreement of Peru, in whose territory the offence was said to have been committed. The Court held that Colombia was not so entitled, and in consequence that Peru was not bound to grant Haya de la Torre a safe-conduct. The Court was then asked to give a second judgement arising from this situation, and held that though asylum had become unlawful, Peru was not entitled to demand surrender. The law's a hass, maybe. But the Court can only answer the questions put to it. If the two countries had only asked for a decision to be given *ex aequo et bono* the situation might have been very different.

The Corfu Channel case was brought by UK against Albania after an explosion of mines in the Channel had caused heavy loss of life and severe damage to two British warships. The Corfu Channel is an international strait, and in time of peace it is customary for warships to proceed through an international strait without asking the prior consent of the coastal state. The Court was not asked to pronounce whether the British warships were entitled to sail in Albanian waters, nor whether Yugoslavia had played any part in the laying of mines, and consequently did not do so. A second question asked by Britain was whether British warships could enter Albanian territorial waters for purposes of mine-sweeping without the consent of Albania. They had in fact done so. To this the Court gave a resounding and unanimous 'No'. 'The Court can only regard the alleged right of intervention as the manifestation of a policy of force such as has in the past given rise to most serious abuses, and such as cannot, whatever be the present defects in international organization, find a place in international law.' But on the main issue they found against Albania. She knew that the minefield existed within her territorial waters and failed to notify other states, and was therefore internationally responsible and under duty to pay compensation.

The Anglo-Norwegian Fisheries case was one of great complexity, though the issue was simple, whether a Norwegian decree of 12 July 1935 delimiting the fisheries zone was in accordance with international law. The British claimed that considerable areas of the high seas were thereby closed to British fishing vessels. It was treated by the Court as an issue concerning the limit of the territorial sea to which Norway was entitled. A majority decision went in her favour, but it was particularly interesting because one of the criteria admitted was that of economic and social need.

In the Morocco Case, two Great Powers, France and the USA were involved: the jurisdiction has not just been between smaller states. The dispute concerned the rights of US citizens in Morocco. The US contended that certain measures taken under the system of exchange control set up in 1939 affect the rights of the US established under treaties with Morocco. France asked the Court to declare that the US was not within its rights in making such a claim, and that American nationals were not entitled to enjoy preferential treatment, and should be subject to laws and regulations in force in Morocco, particularly as regards imports not involving the allocation of non-French currency. The Court rejected the American claim that benefits enjoyed under a most-favoured-nation clause can continue to be enjoyed in perpetuity after the treaties by which the benefits were conferred have been abrogated, and also rejected an argument that such a clause when contained in a treaty with a Moslem state must be given a different interpretation from a similar clause contained in a treaty with a Christian state. This judgement established some major points of international law.

These, and others like them, might not seem earth-shaking events. Still it is important to have a mechanism to resolve these conflicts. The International Court exists to resolve disputes between states where there is a will on the part of the states concerned to solve their problems, even adversely to perceived national interest, short of a war which would or might prove to be even more adverse to national interest. In a world in which war is always a major disaster, and might become the ultimate disaster, this is no small matter, and might become increasingly attractive even to great powers.

Equally important is the fact that the mechanism is there to provide a body which could take on new rôles if the international community so decides. That is, as always, the decisive factor. Every part of the UN is what we are prepared to make it.

What steps forward could be taken? There is no reason in principle why action involving individuals should not come before the World Court. There is no reason why a legal code should not be produced of offences against international order, such as terrorism, drug smuggling and the like, if the states would agree to refer all such cases to the international tribunal. There is no reason why all states should not be invited to agree to accept the verdict of the International Court in any dispute submitted to it by the Security Council or even by any other state. This would be a step forward, though the verdict would be binding only on those countries, and it is unlikely that the major powers would be among them. There are possible developments in such areas as Human Rights,

Diplomatic Law, Legal Aspects of the New International Economic Order.

All in all, the International Court of Justice, with all its limitations, represents one of the most effective of the organs of the UN, and is some ways the one with the greatest potential for the future. Judgement in fifty international disputes is no small matter.

7 Feeding The Hungry

People are hungry—very many people, and very hungry. UNICEF estimate that each year between 15 and 17 million children under five die of hunger or of disease which is fatal because they are hungry. 450,000,000 people are very hungry indeed at any time. When harvests fail the figure is higher.

More people die of starvation every three minutes than died at Hiroshima.

There are a number of false beliefs about this hunger.

It is not true that there is insufficient food to go round. The grain produced, if properly distributed, would give every human being ample protein and more than 3000 calories a day. But a third of the grain produced is fed to animals. There are terrifying anomalies. In 1971 during acute drought the countries of the Sahel actually exported 15 million kilos of vegetables, mainly to Europe. In 1974, after the floods in Bangladesh, people could not afford the rice which was actually available.

It is not true that there is insufficient land. Less than half of the world's arable land is planted. Landowners often prefer to develop export crops. In the 1960s and 1970s in Africa, tea production went up sixfold, coffee fourfold, sugarcane threefold, and cotton and cocoa doubled. But food production for home consumption dropped.

It is not true that hunger results from overpopulation. Brazil has actually more land per person under cultivation than the USA, but the proportion of the population going hungry is increasing. In fact a higher standard of living, dietetically and in other ways, has been shown to reduce the birthrate.

It is not true that food production must be increased at all costs. Great care must be used over new technologies and especially chemical fertilizers and pesticides. It is more important to encourage peasant farming, with more efficient hand-tools. It is not true that it is best for a country to concentrate on a single crop which it is particularly qualified to produce. This is a specious but dangerous view. Mono-culture designed for export leaves hungry countries at the mercy of their own rich, and of price-fixing on the international market.

It is not true that hunger is a competition between the rich world and the poor world. On the contrary, apart from any humanitarian feeling, the Brandt report showed clearly that it is in everyone's material interests to see a higher standard of living in the poorer countries.

The Food and Agriculture Organization (FAO) exists to meet this. Sometimes experts have given wrong advice by exporting their familiar solutions to an inappropriate environment. More often patient steady careful advice has brought staggering improvements. One early piece of work was in Afghanistan where the replacement of the old-fashioned sickle by the modern scythe increased the efficiency of the farmers thirteenfold. Some interesting work has similarly been done on improving the design of the hand trenching-tool widely used in Africa.

A different line of research has been to find strains of rice or maize or other grain which give a higher yield and are more disease-resistant. Cold-resistant, quick-ripening strains of wheat have enabled far more of the chill tundra of Northern Europe and Asia to be brought under cultivation. In fact it was through the FAO that a new strain of maize was introduced into Europe and America giving increased yields of fifty to a hundred per cent. Even in the North we are careless. In 1949 a million tons of sugar beet were lost in Britain to sugar beet 'yellows', though the needful precautions were well-known. Fairfield Osborn tells the story of a farmer who was invited to a lecture on soil conservation and replied: 'There's no use my going to that meeting about farming better. I don't farm as good as I know how to now.'

Another research project has been to check diseases which affect animals. Rinderpest, a cattle disease, destroyed a million buffaloes in China in a year. To a Chinese farmer in those days a buffalo meant about seven tons of grain. An experimental campaign in Thailand eliminated the disease. This is one example of many.

FAO found that one fifth of the total world production of food was being lost to pests—insects, rabbits, locusts, vermin. Even in UK we were losing each year to pests 200,000,000 gallons of milk, one and a half billion eggs, and enough meat to feed 4,000,000 people. Schemes of locust control in Mexico and Central America seem to have been successful, but the indiscriminate use of insecticides did harm as well as good. But the devisal of simple storage devices not accessible to rats was a great boon to Africa.

Another major effort was in irrigation. North Africa was once the granary of the Roman Empire. In North Africa and in the Near East advances were made in some instances by unclogging and redeveloping the channels which the Romans had constructed, and in general by reapplying the same practices. Israel in particular took up the challenge of irrigation with marked vigour and fine enthusiasm. FAO advised on similar schemes in Pakistan and Sri Lanka.

Much else was accomplished in the early years—a comprehensive development plan for Polish agriculture, a mission to Greece aiming to double pre-war production, advice to Venezuela on the production of vegetable oil. And it has all along been international work. In the mid-1950s, George Mulgrue gave a broadcast on the work of FAO and closed with these words:

I think there could be no better illustration of how real this internationalism is than the list of the men who are actually in the field trying to teach the world how to grow more food. In Afghanistan, for instance, there is a Chinese silk man, a Swiss small-tools man, and a Swedish expert in seeds. In Brazil we have a Dutchman, an Australian and a Frenchman; in Burma an Australian and a Japanese. In Ceylon our mission chief is a Canadian, and working with him are a Dutchman, a Finn, a Trans-Jordanian, and a South African. There is a Dane in Chile, a Czech in Ecuador, and an Italian in Honduras. Working in Ethiopia there are a Canadian, a Chilean, a Belgian, an Australian, a Peruvian, a Haitian, and a Swiss. In Haiti, an Israeli, and a Chinese to teach pond fishery. A Yugoslav statistician is helping the Indonesians. There are Frenchmen, Italians, Dutch and Japanese in

Iran. There are Rhodesians, Greeks, Swedes, Triestians, Australians, and Swiss in Libya. And there are Englishmen and Australians nearly everywhere. This is an international attempt to share knowledge so that there shall not be so much hunger in the world.

It was in 1962 that the FAO established the World Food Programme to channel food surpluses from countries which had too much to those which had too little. But this was not idle and indiscriminate charity. Except in emergencies caused by drought or flood, storm or earthquake, insect plague or other disaster, the gifts have been conditional. The object is that the food should be used to encourage projects for social and economic development. It is to help the poorer countries to help themselves. So, it is not allocated in bulk to governments, but always to specific projects. It might be an inducement to workers to join a project, a part payment for their work, or simply a reinforcement of the physical fitness of those developing work important in itself, with potential for the future. The World Food Programme has never operated the projects—it is essential that these are administered by the country concerned or half their value is lost—but it has been careful to evaluate them.

In the early days there were large food surpluses available in North America and Europe, so that the World Food Programme was able to concentrate on what was happening at the receiving end. Naturally there was a certain amount of experimentation, but the Programme took shape with astonishing speed.

Four conclusions emerged:

(a) The most useful projects are labour-intensive without being capital-intensive. Such are schemes for agricultural development, improved irrigation, road-building in rural areas, forestation. Among the most important aspects of this is making possible work during the 'fallow' periods between growing seasons. At these times food reserves are liable to run low, and therefore additional supplies are essential to provide the energy to enable the work to be done.

(b) Great benefit may be gained by resettlement in new areas. But food aid is essential during the period leading up to the first harvest.

55

(c) Increased livestock production can be achieved through the provision of feed for animals.

(d) Less direct, and not easily to be measured, but perhaps most important of all, is the result of ensuring adequate and appropriate food for pregnant mothers and young children.

In all, 155 projects were begun in the first three years. It would of course be nonsense to imagine that they were all unqualified successes. One of the most important aspects of the World Food Programme is the care their people take in recording and in evaluation. The result is that failures may be as important for the future as successes.

One of the great successes of the first three years was in the United Arab Republic. The pasture lands were being overgrazed, the desert was encroaching on once fertile terrain, the nomadic Bedouins were being driven onto less and less suitable land, their animals were dying like flies. The government, in co-operation with FAO, developed a scheme to restore the land, improve the stock and raise the standard of living. But it depended on the Bedouins modifying their traditional way of life. At this point, enter the World Food Programme. They promised that if the Bedouins would leave untouched an area of 100,000 hectares designated for the government scheme, they would compensate with food for the people and feed for the animals. The proposal was greeted with extreme scepticism, but the Bedouins, however reluctantly, agreed to the terms, and as they watched the land developing their doubts were allayed. They themselves asked for the area concerned to be increased fivefold to half a million hectares, and for their children to be enrolled in food education programmes. They accepted professional advice on improving their stock. They even began, of their own volition, to build permanent housing near the developed area.

This was only one of many successes. At the end of three years it was clear that the World Food Programme had come to stay, at least until there was a dramatic change in the economy of the South. Throughout the 1960s the scale of operations and the food pledged by donor countries both expanded enormously. The early 1970s saw a setback, and projects involving animal feeding had for a time to be dropped. But by 1973-4 there was again an increase. A pledging conference is held every two years. Pledges are about two thirds food and one third cash to cover storage and transport costs. The pledging for 1983-4 has a goal over the two years of $1,200,000,000. The pledges do not come only from the rich countries. Countries which are themselves in receipt of help, give to those in greater need when they have food available.

The whole concept of food aid, except in emergencies, has been challenged. It has been said that it depresses the price of local produce, and aggravates the plight of the local farmer, that it may discourge government and farmers from developing their own agriculture, and (though this is a diametrically opposite point) may lead to the dumping of unsuitable goods (wheat for rice-consumers, pigs in Muslim countries). The World Food Programme's answer is that this need not and does not happen if the projects are carefully chosen and evaluated. The proof of the pudding, if one may use the cliché in this connection, is in the eating, and the World Food Programme has not in fact acted as a disincentive to local agriculture.

Its achievements have been staggering. It has been responsible for 1200 projects in 113 countries over 20 years, with a distribution of food valued at over $6,000,000,000. How many millions of people have received food is not known. There have been over one hundred donor countries, and the amount given has risen by nearly 500 per cent during that period.

Today there are projects on every continent, including reforestation in China and Ethiopia; dairy development in Morocco, Mozambique and Nepal; improvement of sanitation in Paraguay; development of food security in Mali; rural resettlement in Sri Lanka; and a school feeding programme in the Gambia.

Two final things about this work. First, it is a work of peace. Nearly two thousand years ago the Roman statesman and philosopher Seneca wrote: 'Justice and Mercy do not live in the hearts of the starving; their thoughts are not guided by reason.' Lord Boyd Orr remarked in 1948, 'Social unrest in Europe to-day is found where food is scarcest and dearest.' The second head of FAO, Norris Dodd, declared that 'starvation is a breeder of misery and the seeds of war.' Montgomery himself at

Blackpool in 1948 said: 'We shall never be free from the threat of war until all the peoples of the earth have enough food and other necessities to make them content.'

But, beyond that, it is a work of humanity. Norris Dodd once said: 'All in all, perhaps the most important work of FAO has been to help develop a world consciousness of the crucial nature of the food problem and what can be done about it, and a world conscience that is increasingly demanding adequate action.' Or, as Boyd Orr put it simply, 'If the Governments cannot agree to feed the world, they cannot agree about anything.' The challenge—and the means to fulfil it—are still with us.

8 Health For All By The Year 2000

Disease has always been man's greatest enemy, even greater than war, at least to the point when man acquired the capability of self-annihiliation in war. More Crusaders died of typhus and the plague before the walls of Jerusalem than in the battles with the Muslims. When the Black Death ravaged Europe in the course of the fourteenth century it destroyed a quarter of the total population. The Great War of 1914 – 18 killed 10,000,000 people in four years, but the influenza epidemic of 1919 – 20 killed 20,000,000 people in two years.

Not merely so. There is an appalling disparity between conditions and resources in different parts of the world.

One example is as telling as a host of statistics. To us in the North, diarrhoea is an occasional inconvenience—no more. But in the South, the poorer half of humanity, more children (over 5,000,000) die of diarrhoea each year than the total number born in the United States, Britain, France, Sweden and the Netherlands put together.

Here, more widely, is how the brilliant journalist Anil Agarwal expresses it: 'Some 250 million people today suffer from filariasis of the Bancroftian variety, and 30 million from the form known as onchocerciasis or river blindness. Some 200 million are infected with schistosomiasis. Each year about 150 million new cases of malaria are registered, and the total number of people infected is believed to be much more. These are just a few of the myriad diseases which affect the people of tropical lands. The scale of this suffering is often missed when quantified in abstract millions. Probably it can be better understood when expressed in the following way: a country as big as the Soviet Union is today suffering from filariasis; a nation of the size of the United States of America is urinating blood because of schistosomiasis;

a population equal to that of Japan, Malaysia and the Philippines put together is sweating and shivering with malaria; and a population equal to that of Iran is suffering from river blindness.' (WHO 81,2)

According to the UN, for every 100,000 people in the world there are 556 soldiers and only one doctor. The comparative figures for a number of countries is interesting.

	Military	Medical
Ethiopia	122	1
Somalia	52.6	1
Laos	36.9	1
Syria	35.4	1
Afghanistan	25.6	1
Qatar	24.9	1
Israel	22	1
Iraq	21	1
China	4.7	1
India	3.2	1
USA	1.5	1
USSR	1.5	1
UK	1	1
Canada	0.38	1

The figures come from the World Health Organization and the International Institute of Strategic Studies. The apparent discrepancy with the other figures is that the second table refers to all medical personnel, not just doctors. It might be said that the poorer countries get their priorities wrong, and that is true. But the richer countries encourage the disproportion by their trade in arms.

Out of many figures which could be quoted, one will serve to show the challenge. In 1975, the Sudan had 171 hospitals, each serving 90,000 people, and 144 health centres, each serving 100,000 people.

This is the situation which the World Health Organization (WHO) was created to meet. It was built on the foundations of an increasing international concern for co-operation in matters of health across the previous half-century. The year 1907 had seen the establishment of the International Office of Public Health. The period between the wars brought the Health Organization of the League and some important sanitary conventions. But WHO was new. It was formed in 1948 on the initiative of Brazil and China. Its constitution is a document of great importance. The whole of the preamble especially merits careful attention and study:

The States parties to this Constitution declare, in conformity with the Charter of the United Nations, that the following principles are basic to the happiness, harmonious relations and security of all peoples:

Health is a state of complete physical, mental and social well-being and not merely the absence of disease or infirmity.

The enjoyment of the highest attainable standard of health is one of the fundamental rights of every human being without distinction of race, religion, political belief, economic or social condition.

The health of all peoples is fundamental to the attainment of peace and security and is dependent upon the fullest co-operation of individuals and States.

The achievement of any State in the promotion and protection of health is of value to all.

Unequal development in different countries in the promotion of health and control of disease, especially communicable disease, is a common danger.

Healthy development of the child is of basic importance; the ability to live harmoniously in a changing total environment is essential to such development.

The extension to all peoples of the benefits of medical, psychological and related knowledge is essential to the fullest attainment of health.

Informed opinion and active co-operation on the part of the public are of the utmost importance in the improvement of the health of the people.

Governments have a responsibility for the health of their peoples, which can be fulfilled only by the provision of adequate health and social measures.

61

The objective is defined as follows in the First Article:

> The objective of the World Health Organisation shall be the attainment by all peoples of the highest possible level of health.

Then follows a definition of the functions of WHO in the Second Article:

(a) to act as the directing and co-ordinating authority on international health work;

(b) to establish and maintain effective collaboration with the United Nations, specialised agencies, governmental health administration, professional groups and such other organisations as may be deemed appropriate;

(c) to assist Governments, upon request, in strengthening health services;

(d) to furnish appropriate technical assistance and, in emergencies, necessary aid upon the request or acceptance of governments;

(e) to provide or assist in providing, upon the request of the United Nations, health services and facilities to special groups, such as the peoples of trust territories;

(f) to establish and maintain such administrative and technical services as may be required, including epidemiological and statistical services;

(g) to stimulate and advance work to eradicate epidemic, endemic and other diseases;

(h) to promote, in co-operation with other specialised agencies where necessary, the prevention of accidental injuries;

(i) to promote, in co-operation with other specialised agencies where necessary, the improvement of nutrition, housing, sanitation, recreation, economic or working conditions and other aspects of environmental hygiene;

(j) to promote co-operation among scientific and professional groups which contribute to the advancement of health;

(k) to propose conventions, agreements and regulations, and make recommendations with respect to international health matters and to perform such duties as may be assigned thereby to the Organisation and are consistent with its objective;

(l) to promote maternal and child health and welfare and to foster the ability to live harmoniously in a changing total environment.

(m) to foster activities in the field of mental health, especially those affecting the harmony of human relations;

(n) to promote and conduct research in the field of health;

(o) to promote improved standards of teaching and training in the health, medical and related professions;

(p) to study and report on, in co-operation with other specialised agencies where necessary, administrative and social techniques affecting public health and medical care from preventive and curative points of view, including hospital services and social security;

(q) to provide information, counsel and assistance in the field of health;

(r) to assist in developing an informed public opinion among all peoples on matters of health.

The constitution defines health positively. It recognizes that health and disease know no frontiers. More, it recognizes that the health of each is the responsibility of all. Today the World Health Organization has over 150 members. Not in those days. But the members bound themselves to work for the eradication of preventable disease among all mankind.

While WHO was still in its preparatory stages, a cholera epidemic broke out in Egypt. It was spreading at the rate of a thousand cases a day. It was checked, confined to Egypt, and brought under control within six weeks, an achievement without parallel in medical history. Thirty-two tons of anti-cholera vaccine and blood serum were shipped by air from seventeen countries, including Australia, Japan, USA and USSR.

In the early days, in addition to its Assembly and Executive, WHO divided the work between six Regional Committees. In Africa there was treatment of bilharziasis, research into yaws, and provision of milk for schools. In the Americas there was need for emergency health services in the wake of the El Salvador earthquake; this apart, there was a primary emphasis on insect control. In South-East Asia priority was given to cutting down infant mortality: Sir Alexander Fleming, the discoverer of pencillin, was one

63

of those who went to India to work on this. It was combined with an emphasis on maternity and child welfare. Malaria, tuberculosis, yaws and the venereal diseases took their toll of millions, and have not yet been overcome. In Europe, where the frontiers are more than ever meaningless in the real world of disease, much was achieved in the eradication of malaria, tuberculosis and other epidemic diseases as well as in insect control. The systematic use of DDT in those days worked wonders, and achieved its primary target. In one year in Greece the incidence of malaria dropped from 85% to 5%. Nineteen forty nine was the first year since Hannibal's invasion that no-one in Italy died of malaria. They used to say that DDT meant *Domani dormiamo tranquilli* ('Tomorrow we sleep soundly'). The Eastern Mediterranean Committee, based in Alexandria, began by systematic factual surveys and careful planning. I have a vivid memory of the results of this when we accidentally encountered a WHO team at work in a hamlet in the wilds of Jordan, and of the little girl who courageously allowed herself to be vaccinated, setting an example to her more timorous elders. The Committee for the Western Pacific similarly were noted for their careful planning.

Part of the most rewarding work of those first years were matters which we today take for granted but at the time required a lot of patient spade-work. For example, on 1 October, 1952 the nations agreed on a single body of international sanitary regulations replacing the sixteen outmoded conventions previously in operation. Again, WHO was responsible for the compilation of an international pharmacopoeia or drug-register. This meant in effect the standardization of drugs and medicine and the technique of recording them throughout the world. This made it far easier to compare and check experiments in different countries. It also made it possible, say, for a diabetic from Birmingham to order his insulin in Bangkok and know that he will receive 'the mixture as before'. A third of these unheralded practical achievements was the publication and circulation of health statistics throughout the world, and greatly improved exchange of medical knowledge.

In the field, the first years saw the vital development of advisory services. In the first year of operation, health missions were sent to Austria, China, Ethiopia, Greece and Poland. From these small beginnings the services reached out all over the world.

Looking more recently at its practical achievements and current fieldwork WHO gave priority to disease control:

Immunization programmes against the six childhood diseases: diphtheria, whooping cough, tetanus, measles, polio, TB.

Research and training on malaria, snail fever, filariasis, leishmaniasis, sleeping sickness, Chagas' disease, leprosy.

International collaborative research programme on **development of health services**, disease control and fertility regulations.

Treatment of acute diarrhoea. More children die each year of diarrhoea than the total number born in USA, UK, France, Sweden and the Netherlands put together.

A new vaccine against meningitis, a major breakthrough in 1974.

The eradication of smallpox worldwide, involving among other things the saving of $1,000,000,000 a year on vaccination.

World influenza outbreaks carefully recorded and countered.

Major campaign against **river-blindness** in seven countries of the Volta river-basin.

Training of health workers and health education to control **venereal diseases**, and international survey of resistance levels to treatment.

Establishment of **International Agency for Research on Cancer**.

Alongside these major campaigns related to particular diseases are the wider campaigns on which health ultimately depends, environmental health, water supply, sanitary services, control of pollution, food hygiene, the effect of pesticides on food, the effect of additives, mental health and psychiatric treatment. WHO has shown a particular concern to make health care available to rural areas and to the inner city. Except in emergencies

WHO does not in general act; it encourages action; it helps people to help themselves. The programme of technical co-operation with governments emphasizes national self-reliance, efficient use of local resources, health promotion, and social justice in the distribution of health services. The aim is to integrate primary health care into an overall development effort, at a cost that the community and nation can afford. Primary health care means: education concerning prevailing health problems and the methods of preventing and controlling them; promotion of food supply and proper nutrition; an adequate supply of safe water and basic sanitation; maternal and child care, including family planning; immunization against the major infectious diseases; prevention and control of locally endemic diseases; appropriate treatment of common diseases and injuries; provision of essential drugs. But WHO insists that these developments must take place through the local communities 'in the spirit of self-reliance and self-determination'. The proclaimed goal is 'Health for All by the Year 2000'.

Sudan may be taken as an example of what can be done, and that despite political troubles. We have noted the poor provision of hospitals and health centres. But over the past ten years primary health care has been given priority, and in most of the eighteen provinces some form of health delivery services is operating at grassroots level. The emphasis is on prevention not cure, on teaching the rural population, including nomads, about hygiene and some simple precautions to avoid the commoner diseases. Active participation from the local community is expected, with contributions in cash, kind or service. Local knowledge often helps: for example, the baobab yields a fruit which is effective against dysentery. The community health workers operate on transport provided by the community: camel or ox or bicycle. Each primary health care unit covers a radius of about ten miles and a population of 4000; five or six of them are linked to a dispensary in a single health care complex. WHO and UNICEF have encouraged and helped to sustain the work.

One of the great undertakings of the 1980s has been the UN Water Decade—or, in full, the International Drinking Water Supply and Sanitation Decade. It is generally accepted that 1,800,000,000 lack reasonable access to clean water, and 2,400,000,000 lack adequate sanitation. The bulk of these are in Asia, Africa and Latin America.

The resultant diseases may be conveniently classified under five heads:

(a) water-borne diseases (e.g. diarrhoea, cholera, typhoid) spread by drinking or other use of contaminated water;

(b) water-washed diseases (e.g. roundworm, whipworm) spread by poor personal hygiene or lack of facilities for disposal of human waste;

(c) water-based diseases (e.g. bilharzia) transmitted by a vector which spends part of its life-cycle in water and enters the human through drinking in water or placing part of the body in it;

(d) water-related diseases (e.g. malaria, river-blindness, sleeping-sickness) which are derived from insects breeding in unhealthy water;

(e) fecal disposal diseases (e.g. hookworm) caused by organisms breeding in excreta.

It is estimated that these five heads underlie 80% of all illness in the Third World, and that 30,000 children die every day as a consequence.

In addition, the availability of water means better irrigation, so more crops and more food. Less disease means more productivity; clean water affects animals as well as humans. All the pointers suggest that better health, longer life expectation and a higher standard of living will lead to smaller families and help to check the astronomical population explosion. This is why the conference at Mar de Plata in 1977, out of which the Water Decade sprang, urged governments to 'adopt programmes with realistic standards for quality and quantity to provide water...by 1990 if possible'.

When the Water Decade was launched, the total cost was estimated at $800,000,000,000 spread across the ten years. That is not a particularly large sum compared with arms expenditure; the annual outlay of $800 billion for the whole world is not very different from the annual arms expenditure of the Far Eastern countries. However, it soon became clear that the rich countries were not prepared to allocate such sums to the real needs, and the UN Development Programme and the World Bank have revised the figures to $300 billion. Present contributions are about $10 billion a year.

This might seem disappointing. In one sense it is. Nonetheless, the original plan was to leap within the decade from nothing to the extravagance we practise in the North. This is clearly undesirable; it would further reduce local involvement and effort and leave rural communities disastrously dependent on remote urban action.

Water-borne sewerage is highly extravagant. In Britain one third of our domestic water is used in water-closets; only one twenty-fifth ministers directly to our lives. In India they aim to provide water-borne sewerage only in towns of 100,000 and over. Smaller communities will have pit latrines and pour-flush latrines. There will be a startling improvement in health conditions at small expense.

In Zimbabwe, a subsistence farmer can erect for himself a much improved pit latrine. The cost of materials comes to about $10, and the latrine will be used by half a dozen or more people.

Wells and boreholes are an important means of access to clean water. In Malawi, wells and boreholes are operated by handpump. Installation runs to about $6 per head among those who use each well, and maintenance should not exceed $50 a year. In Upper Volta, wells have to be sunk to a depth of 30 metres, and lined with reinforced concrete. Even so, the cost is only $11 a head if a bucket is used, and $14 if it is operated by a handpump. The village contributes an initial $145 to cover spares and as a contribution to the wages of a mechanic who will cover fifteen or twenty villages.

To meet the basic minimum aims of the Decade, stand pipes and pit latrines in rural areas, individual taps and sewerage in towns would cost $25m each day through the Decade. That is a lot of money. But the world spends $240m each day on cigarettes and $2,000m each day on arms. We need a sense of proportion.

Health for All by the Year 2000 depends in a real sense on Water for All by the Year 1990.

68

9 Education—In The Widest Sense

The preamble to the charter of UNESCO—United Nations Educational, Scientific and Cultural Organization—is one of the great declarations of the human spirit:

> The governments of the States Parties to this Constitution on behalf of their peoples declare:
>
> That since wars begin in the minds of men, it is in the minds of men that the defences of peace must be constructed;
>
> That ignorance of each other's ways and lives has been a common cause, throughout the history of mankind, of that suspicion and mistrust between the peoples of the world through which their differences have all too often broken into war;
>
> That the great and terrible war which has now ended was a war made possible by the denial of the democratic principles of the dignity, equality and mutual respect of men and by the propagation, in their place, through ignorance and prejudice, of the doctrine of the inequality of men and races;
>
> That the wide diffusion of culture, and the education of humanity for justice and liberty and peace are indispensable to the dignity of man and constitute a sacred duty which all the nations must fulfil in a spirit of mutual assistance and concern;
>
> That a peace based exclusively upon the political and economic arrangements of governments would not be a peace which could secure the unanimous, lasting and sincere support of the peoples of the world, and that the peace must therefore be founded, if it is not to fail, upon the intellectual and moral solidarity of mankind.
>
> For these reasons, the States Parties to this Constitution, believing in full and equal opportunities for education for all, in the unrestricted pursuit of objective truth, and in the free exchange of ideas and knowledge, are agreed and determined to develop and to increase

69

the means of communication between their peoples and to employ these means for the purposes of mutual understanding and a truer and more perfect knowledge of each other's lives;

In consequence whereof they do hereby create the United Nations Educational, Scientific and Cultural Organization for the purpose of advancing, through the educational and scientific and cultural relations of the peoples of the world, the objectives of international peace and of the common welfare of mankind for which the United Nations Organization was established and which its Charter proclaims.

Declarations are important. They recall us to first principles. They challenge us. They form a goal, a vision, a commitment. But what matters is the action that springs from them.

We have largely forgotten the situation which Unesco faced in Central Europe in 1946. One of the first Unesco reports was on 'The Teacher and the Post-War Child in War-Devastated Countries.' Some of the questions asked by the teahcers are a poignant reminder of those terrrible years:

'We have no educational materials. Do you have suggestions for teaching under those conditions?'

'Our children are restless, nervous, irritable. How can we help them to overcome these characteristics?'

'Some of our children seem to take pleasure in destruction. How can we cope with this situation?'

'Our school buildings are destroyed or badly damaged. How can we teach under such conditions?'

'We have very few textbooks for our classes. What can we do under such circumstances?'

'Some of our young people resent and resist the authority of their parents, their teachers and other adults. What can be done to develop respect for authority?'

'Some of our older boys and girls continue to steal, gamble, and indulge in immoral practices. How can we develop in them better standards?'

'We have many children affected with tuberculosis in our schools. What can we as teachers do for them?'

'There are many adults and older young people who had little or no education during the war, who are returning to school but who crowd our limited facilities. How should we handle this situation?'

'Our children are hardened to the fact of death. How can we make them more sensitive to the importance and value of human life and personality?'

There are no easy answers to those questions, but Unesco brought together the people who might work together in seeking ways forward.

Behind this spiritual malaise lay the material destruction left by war. One trivial statistic remains in the mind by reason of its very bizarreness. The city of Budapest alone had as much glass destroyed in bombing and street-fighting as would have paved a road one-and-a-quarter miles wide right across the United States from coast to coast. In Czechoslovakia, three schools out of every five were totally destroyed, and four teachers out of every five were missing. In Poland, nine schools out of ten were closed, most of them destroyed, and nearly half the teachers were missing. Even in Britain, 6000 schools were completely destroyed during the war and 24,000 teachers lost to the teaching profession.

Almost Unesco's first task was to estimate, and find ways of meeting the immediate, basic, material needs: 150 million pencils, 70 million notebooks, 10 million pens, 100 million sheets of writing paper, 40 million sheets of drawing paper, 1 million rulers, 2 million compasses, and other instruments in like quantity. This list embraces the most elementary needs. It does not touch printed textbooks. It does not include buildings. It does not mention laboratories or scientific apparatus. It ignores higher education and the urgent need to build up libraries and supply periodicals. All these challenges were met in due course. First things first. The whole existence of the UN is amply justified by what Unesco did for the children of a war-torn world.

Work of this nature, unhappily, still has to go on in help to refugees, particularly in Palestine, where Unesco has worked closely with UNRWA (United Nations Relief and Works Agency). In 1978-9 the total enrolment was 327,000 boys and girls in 620 schools, 1216 teachers-in-training in 4 colleges, and 3324 students in vocational training centres—a colossal programme in all.

These represent needs resulting from an emergency, though the emergency in Palestine is long-lasting. But mankind as a whole is in a permanent educational emergency. When Unesco was founded, the population of the world was estimated at somewhere round 2,000,000,000. Fifty-five per cent of these could neither read nor write. If Britain were the world, we should have to imagine a situation in which no-one west of the line of the Pennines, no-one in Scotland, Lancashire, Liverpool and Manchester, the Potteries, Birmingham, the West Midlands, Wales, Bristol and the South-West, was literate.

Unesco began by experimenting with a series of pilot projects in areas with different problems. Two of these were especially successful. One was in the Marbial valley of Haiti, with some 30,000 inhabitants, of whom 22,500 were illiterate, an area where economic conditions were among the worst in the world. One immediate discovery was that education in such an area does not begin with teaching people to read and write. It begins with teaching them how to look after their health and how to grow food properly; reading and writing are a by-product of such basic education. The great Latin American educators, Ivan Illich and Paolo Freire, have been proclaiming a similar doctrine—but it began in the Marbial valley. Mponela in what was then Nyasaland, now Malawi, offered a different challenge. The population was about half that in the Marbial valley, a relatively prosperous agricultural community. Here the women played a more prominent part in society, but were largely illiterate. Appropriate methods made more use of modern technology—maps, film strips, posters, mobile cinema vans, radio equipment.

At the same time, Unesco pioneered a series of regional study conferences organized between the representatives of countries with closely similar problems in similar geographical relations. There are here a number of principles of great importance. One is that the North (in the language of the Brandt report) has not got all the answers. Another is that there is a great deal of wisdom and experience within the countries concerned; the

72

important thing is to share it. A third is that education cannot and must not be divorced from life. It is bound up with health, economic conditions, environment.

Developments in Afghanistan were on a larger scale. Ninety per cent of the people were illiterate when Unesco started work there, and Afghanistan was one of fifteen countries selected for Unesco's Experimental World Literacy Programme. This was linked to agricultural development and carried out in co-operation with the Food and Agriculture Organization; it was associated also with the increased use of radio for education, whether for school children or adults. The programme in Afghanistan was designed over the five years 1967-72 to increase primary school enrolment by 40%, middle-school enrolment by 60% and higher school enrolment by 55%, and to increase the number of qualified primary teachers to 6000 in the same period, with the ultimate aim of free universal primary education by 1990. The whole process has been interestingly international. Medicine has a French ambience, economics is German in approach, polytechnics have a Soviet slant, and engineering is American in approach.

Upper Volta was another area which offered a major challenge. Social tradition was opposed to women's education. Less that 10% of the children went to school; there were nearly all boys, and mostly in the towns. Ninety-five per cent of the people live on the land. The work was carefully pioneered with a woman from Senegal as chief technical adviser. Three areas were chosen for pilot projects. Priority was given to securing a safe and adequate water supply through the provision of wells. This reduced the amount of time spent by women in fetching water from long distances, and the loss of time, energy and life through illness. The first essential of education was then in health and hygiene. A further necessity was to improve health through nutrition and a higher standard of living. So a second priority for education was techniques of farming and co-operative organization. Sheer fatigue after a long day in the fields was hampering education; so formal education had to be confined to the dry season. Another problem was that the local languages had not all been transcribed,

73

and this had to be brought about before literacy could be achieved.

Unesco includes the word 'scientific' in its title. The first Director-General was Dr. Julian Huxley, himself a scientist of world standing, and one of the tasks it has set itself is to stimulate the development of the natural sciences throughout the world. The problems and opportunities can be illustrated from a series of meetings in 1978-9. The second conference of Ministers responsible for Science and Technology Policies in the European and North American Region was held in 1978 in Belgrade. The Director-General noted at the time that the Organization was 'the only international institution in which all the countries of Europe and North America can, without exception, work together'. The 33 countries represented hold the bulk of the world's scientific and technological resources, but they noted and agreed to a greater application of scientific and technological effort to development where it is most needed. The same year saw meetings of the Latin American and Caribbean communities in Quito, and of Asia and Oceania in Bangkok. August 1979 in Vienna saw a major gathering of United Nations Conference on Science and Technology for Development, and this is the primary emphasis of this part of the Unesco programme. In the same year, Unesco sent consultants to advise 37 Member States on setting up or making more effective their national science and technology policy-making bodies.

In all this the work in science education is of major importance. At first sight this might seem relatively straightforward. But the design of laboratories for Europe or America may not be appropriate to the tropics. Textbooks of botany filled with plants from temperate zones are useless in other parts of the world. Even at the most elementary level, A may not be for Apple but for Avocado, P not for Pear but for Pawpaw. Sophisticated equipment may not be the best for students who are going to teach in rural areas. Tanzania provides an example: the demonstration secondary schools attached to the University of Dar-es-Salaam were largely equipped by Unesco. Students have the most up-to-date apparatus available. But they also learn to demonstrate equilibrium with a ballpoint pen, a cork and two forks, and can construct a microscope capable of magnifying a hundred times with a glass bead, some strips of wood and a piece of glass.

Science means research, and Unesco has put work and resources into this field. One important aspect has been the work in Oceanography. In 1955 Unesco set up an International Advisory Committee on Marine Sciences, and in 1960 held an Intergovernmental Conference on Oceanographic Research, out of which emerged the Intergovernmental Oceanographic Commission, which now comprises over a hundred countries. It is ironical that in some ways we know more about the surface of the moon than about the oceans which comprise 70% of the earth's surface. It is essential that we pool our resources on this, and Unesco has made it possible to achieve just that. Without this initiative from Unesco there would have been no Convention on the Law of the Sea. One out of many interesting projects was the co-operation with Britain's Open University to provide an intensive audio-visual course on oceanography suitable for developing countries.

The oceans are only a part of what it is fashionable to term the biosphere. One of Unesco's major programmes on a world scale has been on Man and the Biosphere (inevitably MAB). This grew rapidly to embrace about 100 national committees and about 600 field research projects, many of the highest importance. For example, one in Tunisia is seeking to understand and check the encroachment of the desert. One in Indonesia is studying changes in the primary forest. Quite differently, one in Rome has been studying urban ecology, especially in relation to the hinterland.

Unesco's C stands for 'Cultural', and some of the most important work has been to preserve the world's cultural heritage. The best-known operation in this field was the preservation in Nubia of the artistic treasures of twenty temples threatened by the waters of the Aswan Dam, and the rescue and reconstruction, stone by stone and block by block, of the two great Abu Simbel temples. Of equal importance, though less dramatic, has been the saving of the Buddhist temple at Borobudur in Central Java, where monsoon rains had washed away the earth support of the terraces till they leaned crazily outwards and had covered the surface of statues and buildings with edacious moss and lichen. The temple is over a thousand years old, stands on a square base of side 117 metres, rises in four terraces, with six kilometres of wall covered with 1460 carved reliefs, representations of the Buddha's life, and above 72 stupas in concentric rings, each with a statue of the Buddha in meditation. The rescue operation involved dismantling and reconstructing the lower terraces on a concrete raft with adequate drainage, and restoration and protection of the stonework. The Indonesian government has borne most of the expenditure, but a fund established by Unesco will have covered about a third, as well as expert advice. More recently six major monuments in Venice, damaged by flood, have been restored through Unesco. At Carthage in Tunisia Unesco has made possible the preservation of the archaeological remains in a national park. At Herat in Afghanistan, Katmandu in Nepal, Sukothai in Thailand, Tambomachoay in Peru, and in other parts of the world, buildings of major importance have been protected and safeguarded. Bolivia, Chile, Colombia, Ecuador, Peru and Venezuela have been brought together to cooperate in preserving monuments in the Andes. Other important operations have been at Mohendojaro in Pakistan, Gorée in Senegal, Kotor in Yugoslavia after earthquake damage, San Francisco de Lima in Peru, La Plaza Vieja and Havana in Cuba, Wadi Hadramaout and other centres in Yemen, and rock-hewn churches at Göreme in Turkey.

Cultural history is not always visible. Two major undertakings in book form have been *The General History of Africa* and *The History of Civilizations in Central Asia*. Language is a basic expression of culture. T. A. Lamzon's *Handbook of Philippine Language Groups* and R. S. Dandekar's *Modern Trends in Indology* are among publications in this field, and a ten-year project for the Study of Oral Tradition and the Promotion of African Languages is under way. There has been a symposium in Tahiti on the Preservation and Promotion of Polynesian Languages. Theatre too is an important expression of artistic creativity, and Unesco's African Theatre Workshop, held in Ghana, was a notable example of encouraging a traditional culture to be aware of, but not swamped by, modern technology. Another, different example is the recording of the Elche Mystery Play from Spain on film. Museums form another area where Unesco has been active in conferences, publications and advice. A museum should be an exhibition of living culture, a Temple of the Muses. It became for many a dead and dusty grave of the past. But modern techniques have brought it alive again, and Unesco has made it possible to use museums constructively throughout the world, to preserve culture without mummifying it.

Less easily definable is the contribution Unesco makes directly to peace. In general, the co-operation of the nations for positive ends is wholly commendable, but Unesco meetings of recent years have sometimes been used for political posturing rather than cultural co-operation, and this instead of the very real achievements has hit the headlines. More directly, we should not forget some of Unesco's early initiatives—the Unesco clubs, often springing up spontaneously in schools and youth organizations; the Associated Schools Project encouraging special programmes in education on world problems and international co-operation, the study of other peoples and other cultures and human rights; the Unesco Coupon Scheme enabling people in soft currency areas to buy books, films and scientific equipment from hard currency areas; the Unesco Gift Coupons enabling ordinary citizens to help to provide necessary equipment in poorer areas of the world; publication of *Study Abroad* and *Vacation Study Abroad*.

More recently we may note the establishment in 1978 of the Simon Bolivar International Prize, to be awarded 'to persons who have made an outstanding contribution to the freedom, independence and dignity of peoples and to the strengthening of solidarity among nations, fostering development and facilitating the quest for a new international economic, social and cultural order'. In the same year, the General Conference unanimously adopted the Declaration on Fundamental Principles concerning the contribution of the Mass Media to Strengthening Peace and International Understanding, to the Promotion of Human Rights and to Countering Racialism, Apartheid and Incitement to War, a statement of major importance, backed by practical measures to facilitate the flow of information, and improve conditions for rural radio in Jamaica, the rural press in Tanzania, educational radio in Cape Verde, journalism in Nigeria, District Information Officers in Zambia, television training in Bangladesh, and much else.

The Director-General, in his address to the Unesco Board in September 1982, outlined the achievement of the past four months. Because this is a relatively short space of time, an account of those activities gives some indication of the widespread work of Unesco. In the Near East, 643 schools were operating in conjuction with the UN Relief and Works Agency for Palestine Refugees. Nearly 10,000 teachers were serving 339,000 pupils. Training schools covered a further 5000 students, and there was provision for 340 fellowships for university study each year. This alone would be a major achievement.

There had been major concern for the preservation and rehabilitation of the cultural heritage. A project to control the water level in Venice by closure of the lagoon entrances had now been approved. Initiatives had been taken with the Government of Cyprus and representatives of the Turkish community to preserve and secure the monuments there. There had been a special mission to Tyre, and discussion with the authorities of Lebanon and Israel about its protection. Angkor Wat was in danger, and Unesco was acting urgently with those responsible in Bangkok. A special mission had gone to Iran at the government's invitation to see and advise on the treasures there.

There had been special activity in the marine sciences, as the five-yearly conference had been held in August. The new Convention on the Law of the Sea is of the highest importance in this field. Unesco had undertaken to have an oceanographic vessel built for the University of Qatar.

As always, there had been major international conferences, some regional, some global. Regional conferences covered education and economic development in Africa, educational innovation in the Caribbean and a major project in Latin America and the Caribbean. Worldwide conferences included the Round Table on Youth in the 1980s, the meeting of experts on the teaching of human rights, the Second World Conference on Cultural Policies,

78

the World Congress on Books, the International Congress on the Universal Availability of Publications, and the committee of governmental experts to deal with the intellectual property aspects of the protection of the expressions of folklore. We can see in these meetings the importance of helping nations with similar problems to work together, the amount of work needed to make possible things we take for granted, such as the availability of publications, and, in the last meeting, the need for international agreement on what is in fact an exceedingly complex legal problem. The meetings were held all over the world, Paris and Geneva, Harare, Bridgetown and St. Lucia and Mexico City, Costinesti in Romania.

The Director-General had given a major address to the Special Session of the UN General Assembly devoted to disarmament. The first such special session had charged Unesco with four fields of work—information, studies and research, co-operation with non-governmental organizations, and disarmament education. He highlighted some of the work undertaken, especially the World Congress on Disarmament Education, the training seminar in disarmament for university teachers in Latin America and the Caribbean, and the symposium on 'Scientists, the arms race and disarmament,' which had produced a series of concrete recommendations. 'Unesco,' he said 'indeed considers that its prime responsibility is to take, within its fields of competence, whatever action may help to reduce international tensions and may be conducive to the maintenance of peace and to disarmament. Standing at the crossroads of all activities of the mind, receptive to all works that express the sensitivities of the peoples, it is constantly attentive to the world, endeavouring to feel its every heartbeat. It is therefore well aware that we live in a world increasingly overshadowed by anxiety: anxiety among the rich at the extent of a rising unemployment which may become the source of grave social tensions, of fear, selfishness and, alas, even of chauvinism; anxiety among the poor, who see more and more doors closed to them and whom relationships of inequality condemn to remain in apparently inescapable situations; and the anxiety felt in many countries at the worsening of tensions, the proliferation of conflicts, and the rise of perils that may lead towards a nuclear war.' He spoke of the concern of intellectuals and scientists, of the way vast resources are squandered to no purpose, adding not to security but to insecurity, of the arms trade which his conscience called him to denounce. He affirmed, 'A peace movement unprecedented in history must now develop everywhere, a movement which insists on collective responsibility for the fate of mankind, a responsibility which must transcend the frontiers of selfish interest and scale the heights of human solidarity.'

In addition to the work of his representatives the Director-General had personally and officially visited the Ukraine, USA, Canada, UK, Greece, Angola, Zaire, Zimbabwe, Grenada, St. Lucia, Jamaica, Mexico, Brazil and Bulgaria.

At the same meeting of the Board, Dr. M'Bow outlined a Medium-Term Plan for Unesco. He identified five tasks, and thirteen major programmes to fulfil them.

The first task is to continue and carry further the appraisal of the world situation. Major Programme I consists in **Reflection on world problems and studies which look to the future**.

The second task is to help establish the conditions for the widest possible participation of individuals and groups in the life of the societies to which they belong and in that of the world community. Major Programme II may be entitled **Education for All** and calls for the eradication of illiteracy and the democratization of education. Major Programme III, **Communication in the service of man**, aims to improve the free flow of information, and to spread books, radio, TV and the press more widely and more freely.

The third task is to strengthen throughout the world the capacity to tackle problems by improving knowledge and know-how (**des savoirs et des savoir-faire**) and spreading these more fairly. This requires four major programmes. Major Programme **IV, The formulation and application of education policies**, lays stress on the educational sciences. Major Programme V, **Education, Training and Society**, involves the social sciences. It is subdivided into six points: education, culture and communication; development of up-to-date technical education as a part of general education; links between education and the world of work; physical education and sport; the contribution of higher education to social progress; relations between education, training and research. Major Programme VI concerns **The sciences and their application to development**. Major Programme VII has to do with **Information systems and access to knowledge**.

The fourth task is to help facilitate the necessary changes and transitions in the various societies. Major Programme VIII deals with **Principles, methods and strategies of action for development**; this is important and breaks fresh ground. Major Programme IX is **Science, technology and society**. Major Programme X, **The human environment and terrestrial and marine resources**, 'seeks to help to bring about the necessary changes in regard to the environment and the rational management of natural resources'.

Finally, the fifth task is concerned with values, peace and respect for human rights. Major Programme XI, **Culture and the future**, aims at a renewal of cultural life, promoting the creative affirmation of identity and encouraging the mutual enrichment of different cultures. Major Programme XII works for **The elimination of prejudice, intolerance, racism and apartheid**. The theme of Major Programme XIII is **Peace, mutual understanding, the freedom of the peoples and human rights**. This incorporates work for the specially disadvantaged, the urban poor, the rural poor, migrant workers, and women.

In 1983, the USA announced its intention to withdraw from Unesco; in 1984, the UK made a similar announcement.

In this situation a number of points must be made.

First, no question but that the administration of Unesco could be improved and economies achieved. Constructive criticism, such as has been made by the British Government, can be heartily welcomed and considerable efforts have been made in response. It is far better to remain inside an organization and work for reform from within.

Second, universality of membership is strongly to be desired.

Third, the USA and UK have been put out by the strength of the voices from the Third World. But they represent the majority of the human race, and we had better listen to them,

81

even if they do not see international organizations the way we do. We can hardly complain that Unesco is dominated by the Third World when 62.8% of the staff come from North America and Western Europe!

Fourth, all the nations have depended to an unhealthy extent on US money for the running of the UN. In the end he who pays the piper is always liable to call the tune and to withdraw if his tune is not played for the dance. The US paid 25% of Unesco's budget—too high a proportion.

Fifth, a great deal of attention has been paid to the so-called New International Information Order, which was alleged to infringe against freedom of speech. It was designed to redress a balance. The international news media are controlled from the 'North'. The 'South' is inadequately represented, inadequately reported and often misreported. This is not in dispute, and those who reject the Order should offer alternative remedies. But what is the New International Information Order? It is the subject of a report by a Commission chaired by Sean McBride, and representative of all parts of the globe. The report has been submitted, democratically discussed, and criticized. It is not part of Unesco policy at all!

Sixth, it should be observed that one of the major pieces of Unesco's work relates to international copyright. It is at least arguable that citizens of nations which withdraw from Unesco should not benefit under agreements organized through Unesco.

Seventh, Britain gains at least as much from Unesco as we put in, on the most selfish materialistic calculation. Our share of the budget is about £4 million a year. Direct purchase of equipment for field projects from Britain by Unesco amounted to over £2 million in 1985. Training of high level professionals in UK under Unesco auspices amounts to about £750,000 a year. In addition we received just under 600 Unesco scolarship holders in the three-year period 1981-3. In 1985 10% of consultants on Unesco field projects came from Britain. Further, those who have trained in this country or worked with British consultants are more likely to purchase British-made equipment in the future. It is singularly short-sighted to withdraw from any part of the international community without a very careful calculation of gains and losses.

Eighth, we should not forget our traditional associations: Julian Huxley was the first Director-General and Joseph Needham the first Assistant Director-General for Science. The American Luther Evans was an early Director-General.

Ninth, when all is said about bureaucracy and mismanagement (and no-one seeks to defend these), the achievements are staggering. Between 1979 and 1983 Unesco carried out over a thousand operational projects in nearly one hundred member states, in addition to several hundred other projects for which it provided expert advice: these range from educational planning and reform in an African country to the restoration of a Buddhist temple and the construction of an oceanographic research ship. It was involved in campaigns which brought literacy to over 15,000,000 adults and children with no access to schools. It helped in the training of about 30,000 teachers in one year. It has raised $40,000,000 to safeguard historic monuments, Venice, the Athens Acropolis, the Havana Plaza Vieja, the island of Gorée, Sri Lanka's Cultural Triangle. It fostered scientific co-operation and scientific congresses.

These things are not negligible, and must not be allowed to fail.

M. Mitterand, President of the French Republic, speaking at the inaugural session of the Unesco General Conference in 1983, stressed that Unesco had fulfilled its mission. He cited its accomplishments, particularly in the field of literacy and the preservation of the universal heritage. It had conferred on environmental research the patent of nobility, he said, and promoted the rebirth of cultural identities. He went on: 'In thirty-eight years, to have developed education, promoted scientific co-operation, preserved our heritage and always to have kept alive the flame of interchange between all the countries of the world—who can improve on that?'

So Unesco must go forward. A recent report has every page headed PEACE, EIRENE, SHALOM, PACE, PAIX, MIR, PAZ, PAX, FRIEDEN, SALAMA, JAAM, and sometimes hieroglyphics which an ignorant Englishman cannot read but

rejoices to see, knowing that they spell out the same message.
We may recall the words of Longfellow:

> Were half the power that holds the world in terror,
> Were half the wealth bestowed on camps and courts,
> Given to redeem the human mind from error,
> There were no need of arsenals or forts.

Unesco has not been given the resources for that. Considering
its limited resources, its achievements are astonishing.

10 Towards A New International Economic Order

The world population is 4.8 billion, of whom three-quarters live in the poor countries. At present rates of growth it is expected that by 2000 the population will be between 6 and $6^{1}/_{2}$ billion, of whom four-fifths will be in the poor countries. In 2050, the population may be 10 billion with 85% in the poor countries. In the poor countries half the population are under twenty. Those who suffer from excessive malnutrition in their first year are liable to be retarded mentally.

The rich countries consume 80% of the world's resources, including half the world's food. They eat five times as much per head as the poor countries. They enjoy 80% of the world's income, produce 90% of the world's manufactures, and do 90% of the world's research, mostly in their own interests.

The number of deaths under one year per 1000 live births is 9 in Sweden, 16 in UK, 17 in Australia and USA, 28 in USSR, but 100 in Egypt, 122 in India, 124 in Pakistan, 133 in Rwanda, 142 in Malawi, and 159 in Liberia. Average life expectancy in UK is 73, in Japan 76, in Angola 41, in Mali or Upper Volta 42. Of the world's children, 15,500,000 die before the age of 5; 15 million of them in the poorer countries. In many of these a third of all children die before the age of 5.

1,500,000,000 people are marginalized, living lives of abject poverty; 800 million are destitute, 500 million are seriously malnourished. 1,000,000,000 have worms inside them. Three-fifths do not have safe drinking water, three-quarters no adequate sanitation. In 1977 the National Academy of Sciences in the USA indicated that 750,000,000 people have incomes of less than $75 a year.

The UN has identified 30 countries as 'Least Developed'; their combined population is somewhat over 250 million. Per capita income is low, literacy less than 20%, manufacturing less than 10% of the Gross Domestic Product, economic growth virtually nil. The situation is particularly acute for countries with no access to the sea. Of nineteen such countries fifteen are among the Least Developed, forming one half of these.

One example may bring things home more than may statistics. Stanley Mooneyham of World Vision visited Sebastian and Maria Nascimento in Brazil. He found a lean-to consisting of one room, with sand floor and thatched roof. The only furniture was a single stool, a charcoal hibachi and four cots covered with sacks containing a little straw. The father was out of work, trying to pick up a few coppers shining shoes. The twins, three years old, were both dying of malnutrition. The two-year-old boy was lying severely retarded by marasmus. The mother was in despair. Mooneyham's comment was 'Tears must be the vocabulary of the anguished soul.' The nourishment in the food we give to our cats and dogs is more than the poor enjoy in Brazil. But there is enough for all if we have the will to share.

A cartoon in *Development* shows a mediaman with microphone and battery-operated cassette-recorder, asking a black child 'What exactly causes hunger?' and receiving the answer 'No food.'

As more of the former colonial dependencies became independent they were at first concerned with raising world public opinion against the relics of colonialism, and between 1960 and 1964 were remarkably successful in making colonialism the uppermost concern of the UN, winning the world as a whole to see the need for a more equitable political order, and turning rhetoric into effective action. This battle largely won, they turned to the attempt to mediate in the interests of peace, notably in the Korean War. But this plunged them into controversy and lack of success, and they realized that numbers are not to be equated with political power, and resolved to be non-aligned between the two great power-blocs. They had an effective voice in the Assembly, but not in the Security Council, where political power lay, or in ECOSOC. They further came to see that economic exploitation was a form of neo-colonialism.

As early as 1960 Zulfiqar Al Bhutto, then delegate for Pakistan, stated to the General Assembly:

> There are two aspects of this difference in the standards of living which are of crucial importance to the world today; first that the disparity is not only great but growing; and, secondly, that the peoples of the underdeveloped countries, living so long at levels of bare survival, are no longer prepared to accept such conditions of life as immutable. A revolution of rising expectations is sweeping through these countries. Fatalism and resignation have given way to expectation and demand.

At first the underdeveloped countries set great store on aid. Aid still offers vital potential. But as aid was not forthcoming on the needed scale, they turned to the UN rather than the individual nations to take the initiative in reducing the gap between rich and poor nations, and in improving conditions of trade.

There had already been an attempt to create a Special Fund for the needs of developing countries. It is characteristic of the history of the UN that a group of experts convened by the Secretary-General proposed such a fund as early as 1949. But the UN cannot act until the nations are willing to act, and negotiations dragged on for nearly ten years in face of opposition from UK, USA and France. The Afro-Asian and Latin American states were the strongest pressure group, only Turkey (under pressure from the USA), Thailand and Liberia not offering support. The Soviet bloc abstained. By 1957, France and the Soviet bloc had come round, and in 1958 the resolution to establish a Special Fund was passed. It was an act of major importance. The UN publication *Basic Facts About the United Nations* put it in a nutshell: 'Established in 1958, the Special Fund is the largest United Nations programme of technical co-operation. The Fund helps low-income countries to develop, in particular by creating conditions that make capital investment feasible or more effective.... The United Nations and its related organizations act as executing agencies for projects assisted by the Special Fund.' But the intense opposition received from the richer countries, largely in the interests of 'private enterprise', persuaded the poorer countries that they must seek a more radical and comprehensive solution. This lay in the attempt to establish a New International Economic Order.

The first step towards this was the establishment of the United Nations Conference on Trade and Development in 1964. UNCTAD seemed to offer hope to the less developed countries, especially when the second session, at New Delhi in 1968, favoured a multilateral non-reciprocal tariff preferred scheme to favour imports of semi-processed and processed products from the poorer countries into the richer (despite a host of limitations and exceptions). The 'haves' continued to cling to their privileges and drag their feet. The energy crisis of 1973 made it clear to rich and poor alike that something must be done.

It was at a special session in the spring of 1974 that the General Assembly declared that the international economic order itself must be changed or the gap between developed and developing countries would continue to widen. The Assembly adopted a Declaration calling for the establishment of a new international economic order, based on equity, sovereign equality, interdependence, common interest and cooperation among all States, which would eliminate inequalities and ensure development. Such a change would require the industrial countries to make adjustments in their policies so as to benefit the poorer countries, which in turn would take steps to promote collective self-reliance and co-operation among themselves. The British delegate commented 'Things will never be the same again.' The Americans, originally strong in criticism of the proposal, came round to a more considered view: 'We in the industrialized world have received fair notice that we must co-operate in working out a more equitable distribution of the world's bounty, or risk finding ourselves isolated in a world of hostile nations and desperate men.'

Associated with the Declaration was a Programme of Action which set out a series of specific measures relating to problems of primary commodities and raw materials, trade, restrictive business practices, industrial production, international monetary reform, and the transfer of science and technology, among many others.

The primary UN organ promoting social and economic progress is the UN Development Programme (UNDP), which works in close co-operation with twenty-six UN-related agencies and institutions, with the regional commissioners, and with the Governments concerned. It is the world's largest single source of multinational technical co-operation aid, carrying out projects which help the countries to attract capital investment needed for rapid progress and to use all available resources as effectively as possible. It should be made clear that recipient governments have provided about 58% of the project expenditure.

UNDP supports about 3500 projects each year in over 150 countries and territories. The countries themselves pay a little over half the costs involved. Here are some of the achievements:

(a) Meeting shortages of raw materials. Reaching untapped energy reserves e.g. geothermal energy. Finding untapped resources — bauxite in the South Pacific, iron ore in Bolivia and Guinea, uranium in Somalia, copper in Mexico. UNDP has discovered resources in industrial minerals valued at $45,000,000,000.

(b) Helping nations to mobilize development capital from both domestic and external sources. UNDP has stimulated $30,000,000,000 in follow-up investment.

(c) Stimulating the growth of local technological capabilities.

(d) Improving standards of living, especially through housing and community development.

(e) Developing new employment opportunities, particularly for young people. UNDP is careful to build labour-intensive enterprises involving only limited capital and technology. They also equip men and women with new skills. A single project trained two million people for 350 occupations.

(f) Helping to increase industrial production, so that the poorer countries can raise their proportion of world production above the present 10%. Encouraging decentralization of industry into rural areas.

(g) Contributing to agricultural productivity. This is the largest single component of UNDP activity. Among other things UNDP has located hundreds of millions of cultivable acres, and hundreds of millions of cubic feet of water for irrigation.

(h) Helping developing countries increase their exports by training specialists in tariff negotiations, marketing, trade planning, international shipping practice and the like.

A few actual projects—a tiny fraction of the whole—will show what can be done:

(a) To meet acute food deficits in Tanzania's offshore islands of Zanzibar and Pemba, which import 40 million pounds of rice a year. — Hydrological surveys, soil tests, and trials with 3000 varieties of rice have enabled 1000 farmers to use 50 highyield strains and have brought 1000 acres under irrigation.

(b) To accelerate Egypt's industrial growth through improved steelmaking. — Technical advice and practical adjustments enabled Egyptian Iron and Steel Co. to raise output by 20%, reduce pollution and lower costs. In 1981 the Company for the first time met its production targets and reported profits.

(c) To strengthen the economy of Honduras with special reference to woodlands. — Establishment of Forestry Management Units taking a holistic approach, plans for reforestation, cleaning and thinning out and planting, growth of 100,000,000 seedlings, adequate fire prevention, development of sawmills.

(d) To raise nutritional standards in Sri Lanka. — Initial feasibility demonstrations encouraged soybean as a cash crop. Cultivation was multiplied 3000%. Soybeans provided a whole range of new foods, including a substitute for coconut milk making it possible to increase the export of coconuts.

(e) To break transport bottlenecks in Brazil, an area larger than Western Europe with only a quarter of the railways. — Training of 3000 aircraft technicians.

(f) To help Mozambique attain greater self-sufficiency in minerals. — Systematic surveys suggest reserves of 50,000,000 tons; this has been followed by advice on the economic potential.

(g) To solve housing crises among Haiti's urban slums. — Grant for 1000 new housing units with water systems, fire precaution, street-lighting and improved sewerage, together with a health centre and nutrition centre.

Among associated programmes are the Revolving Fund for Natural Resources Exploration, which helps to underwrite the exploration of mineral deposits, requiring repayment only when production is economically viable; UN Capital Development Fund, mostly operating on a grant basis not by loans, solely in the least developed countries, 80% in rural areas, directing support to the genuinely poor, and providing 'seed money' for low-cost housing, basic agricultural equipment, irrigation and food-storage systems, cottage industry centres, village schools, vocational training facilities, health clinics, and feeder roads; UN Sahelian Office in view of the special needs of that drought-stricken area; UN Volunteers, 300 of whom in 1977 were serving in 48 countries.

One important pressure point has been over the need for commodity agreements and for a Common Fund to finance the establishment and maintenance of buffer stocks of ten core commodities—cocoa, coffee, copper, cotton, jute, rubber, sisal, sugar, tea and tin. In this way prices can be stabilized. This is obviously in the interest of the less developed countries: to take one example, Ghana has to produce many times the quantity of cocoa to buy a tractor compared with thirty years ago. But it is also in the real interests of the developed countries, and one of the features of international politics over the last two decades is the extent to which Western opinion has become more widely (though not universally) persuaded of this. In 1979, an agreement was established to set up a Common Fund on a modest scale. Further, the voting rights were not based on the size of the financial contributions, but the poorer nations, represented by the so-called Group of 77, were given 47% of the votes. It has proved difficult to implement even this modest proposal. The 1983 UNCTAD VI conference was from the viewpoint of the Third World (to use Alfred Sauvy's phrase) a failure. The USA was intransigent, and the USSR made political capital out of this without being helpful. However, there were positive results. North and South, East and West were in communication. The South saw the need for solidarity among themselves. All realized our interdependence. It is sad to record that in 1985 the Geneva talks on stabilizing the price of cocoa collapsed. The USA, the largest consumer, showed no interest. The UK proposed 100 cents a pound, the producers 135. Rene Montes of Guatemala tried to achieve a compromise at 115, but failed. The economies of Brazil, Ghana and the Ivory Coast are deeply affected by this, but the richer countries show little active concern. The UN provides the instrument, but we still have to use it.

IFAD (the UN International Fund for Agricultural Development) was set up after the 1974 World Food Conference. It has had two great strengths in its operations: it has concentrated on the people really in need and has helped the small landholder and landless from labourers in poor countries, and it has been the only international organization where OPEC and Western nations share the funding. Since it began making its first loans in 1978 it has funded projects to provide for these poorest farmers seeds, fertilizer, tools, irrigation, storage facilities, access roads, all in the spirit that people will be helped only if they share in the planning and the carrying out of the plans. In the period 1978-85 IFAD has financed 152 projects in 83 countries—36% in Africa, 28% in Asia, 19% in Latin America, 17% in the Near East—and when these projects are completed they will increase agricultural yields by 20 million tons of grain each year, making up a quarter of the 1981 cereal deficit in all developing countries. These projects are cost-effective. $200 will enable a small landholder to produce 1 ton of food each year for the rest of his life: it costs twice as much as that to supply 1 ton of food as emergency relief.

But despite this, IFAD faces financial problems. For 1979-81 it was funded at $1,000m, from 1982-4 at $1,100m. But from 1985-7 the funding has been cut to $730m. Of the past funding, 12 OPEC countries contributed 42% and 20 western nations 58% (12:20:: 37.5:62.5). With the fall in oil prices OPEC asked for a 40:60 division. OPEC offered to give $295m if the West would give $465m (roughly 38:62). The West tried to keep their figure down to $415m (42:58 again; but a cut overall of over 35%). As so often, we see that the UN provides an instrument. The nations themselves decide whether they will use it properly.

Aid must be a significant element in changing the pattern of the world economy. The UN has suggested that the 'haves' should offer 0.7% of their Gross National Product (GNP) in Aid. Only four countries have achieved this—Norway 1.06%, Netherlands 0.91%, Sweden 0.85%, Denmark 0.73%. France hopes to reach the target by 1988. The UK has stated its desire to reach the target, but has put no date upon it, and the current trend is downwards, on the most favourable figures 0.43% in 1981, 0.37% in 1982, and 0.35% in 1983. It is no great consolation that the figures for USA and USSR are even lower. It is worth reflecting that at the time of Marshall Aid the US was putting 2.86% of its GNP into overseas aid. Further the British figures for overseas aid for 1981 were £1082m plus £659m in private investment, which is the channel through which the government of the day prefers Britain to act. But private investment is not disinterested, and in 1981 the excess of receipts was £5580m, consisting of £4543m trading profit and £1037m interest on investments. So that the actual flow is in the other direction. Much more needs to be done. The UN sets the target; it is for the nations to fulfil it.

In fact the problem of world debt is staggering. The figures quoted by the Morgan Guarantee Trust Co. for the end of 1982 for the major debtor nations and their debts is as under, in billions of dollars:

Brazil	87	Philippines	16.6
Mexico	80.1	DDR	14
Argentina	43	Peru	11.5
South Korea	36	Tanzania	9.9
Venezuela	28	Nigeria	9.3
Israel	26.7	Hungary	7
Poland	26	Zaire	5.1
USSR	23	Zambia	4.5
Egypt	19.2	Bolivia	3.1
Yugoslavia	19		

This means that for the three at the top of the list, and one or two of the others, the interest due in 1983 was higher than the nation's total annual exports. This becomes virtually meaningless, and there will have to be adjustments, and these can be made only through an international organization, that is the United Nations. Another table of figures shows how the problem has grown for Third World countries.

	1970	1983
Total debt	$68.4 billion	$595.8 billion
Ratio of debt to GNP	13.3%	26.7%
Ratio of debt to exports	99.4%	121.4%

Among the recommendations of the Brandt Report, in addition to the stabilization of prices of primary commodities was the need for the Third World countries to have a greater say in the direction of the International Monetary Fund. At present, control is firmly with the developed countries, and the less developed countries have often claimed that the IMF is insufficiently sensitive to their needs, and that the poorer countries should receive 'positive discrimination'. The richer countries have argued that the IMF is a financial institution providing facilities for all member-states, regardless of their stage of development. To the Third World this is a formula for enabling the rich to be protected while the poor are unprotected. There is a genuine conflict of concept here, but the recommendations of the Brandt Committee must carry a good deal of weight. Again, we see that the UN provides machinery; its use for the greatest good of the greatest number depends upon the will of its members.

The proponents of the New International Economic Order would like to see changes in the World Bank, with increases in its capital base, new facilities and softer terms. The World Bank has on the whole, and perhaps inevitably, operated within the framework of international capitalism, and it has been conservative in its attitudes. Yet one of the most impressive features of the international scene has been the way two successive Presidents of the World Bank (who have to be American), Robert MacNamara and A. W. Clausen, both thought to be inflexibly right wing on their appointment, have, as conscientious holders of a highly responsible office, become outspoken exponents of the need for radical change in order to help the poor of the earth.

Finally, let us revert to the matter of world population.

According to the World Bank the population explosion, in millions (mentioned earlier), can be estimated as follows:

	1960	*1984*	*2025*
World	3,037	4,750	8,297
China	688	1,029	1,409
India	435	750	1,311
Europe	425	490	540
USSR	214	275	339
USA	181	236	286
Nigeria	52	97	329
Egypt	26	46	86

Another way of expressing the startling, astronomical growth is to look at the years it takes to add a billion people to the world's population.

	Years Required	Year Reached
First billion	10,000+	1830
Second billion	100	1930
Third billion	30	1960
Fourth billion	15	1975

| Fifth billion | 11 | 1986 |
| Sixth billion | 9 | 1995 |

In Mexico City the population in 1951 was 3.1m; today it is perhaps 17m: by 2000 it is expected to reach 26m. Only in Thailand has there been a real effort to face that challenge. Their secret is 4000 village health centres served by 220,000 paramedics. The World Bank says that the expenditure of a mere $7.6 billion a year, about 1% of arms expenditure, would achieve a real curb on population growth by 2000. Again and again we see that the United Nations is a resource by which world problems can be solved, but unless the nations are prepared to use that resource the problems will continue.

Ultimately humanity is the endangered species. It need not be. It must not be.

11 Refugees

A refugee is a person who 'owing to well-founded fear of being persecuted for reasons of race, religion, nationality or political opinion, is outside the country of his nationality and is unable or, owing to fear,...is unwilling to avail himself of the protection of that country'. Ever since the First World War, there has been a world problem over refugees. Before 1914 there were refugees enough, but they were able to cope better than today. For one thing travel was easier; you could pass the length and breadth of Europe without a passport. After 1914-18 governments hardened in their attitudes. Refugees had no rights. The League of Nations established its own High Commissioner for Refugees, Fridtjof Nansen, explorer, scholar, statesman and humanitarian. His three rules of life served him well. They were—'Never take a decision through fear; you are never so likely to be wrong.' 'Never leave a line of retreat. Always go forward.' 'The difficult is what takes a little time. The impossible is what takes a little longer.' Nansen operated within strict limits: (a) International action is needed. (b) A permanent organization is not needed. (c) International financial support should be confined to the administration needed; support to the refugees must be given by governments and voluntary agencies. (d) Refugees who are to receive international aid must be clearly defined and identified. These limits were probably necessary and not at the time unduly restrictive. Nansen is remembered as the man who gave refugees hope and the stateless identity.

After the Second World War, experience brought changes, the limitations were impracticable, and the problem of aid massively greater. Europe was a mass of refugees. UNRRA (Relief and Rehabilitation Administration) first took up the work; by 1947 an International Refugee Organization was constitutionally established. In its first five years it repatriated 70,000 refugees and found new homes for 1,100,000 more.

These are statistics. Robert Mackie, Director of the World
Council of Churches Department of Inter-Church Aid and Service to Refugees, gave a salutary reminder to think of individuals.
'When I am tempted to think of refugees in categories,' he wrote,
'—DPs, hard-core, expellees, persecutees, escapees—and all
the horrible words we invent, I try to stop and remind myself
of a day in June, 1940, when, with my wife and son, I was part
of the rabble on the roads of France. My personal papers were
a liability; my handful of banknotes no one would accept; I had
only the clothes I stood up in, and was glad to doss down on a
heap of straw in a corner of a schoolroom floor.' He told how in
his later work on behalf of refugees he met a woman just arrived
in Western Germany, who turned away from him and covered her
face with shaking hands. The interpreter explained, 'She is afraid
you will ask her questions. She has been a refugee four times since
1942, and she lost her only child, frozen to death on one of her
flights. She has had enough questions. Would you like to meet
another refugee in the next room, please?' We must think what
it meant to that woman to find eventual security. Then we can
multiply that thousands—no, millions of times.

Here is an actual scene from those early days. It is on the
quayside at Naples. A ship has come into the harbour, and on
the dockside is standing a woman with a ten-year-old boy. A man
comes down the gangplank. His eyes fall on the boy without interest, then on the woman. He stares for a moment and falls into her
arms. They were two Poles. The mother and her newly born child
were caught up in the German invasion of Poland in 1939. She
had been taken as forced labour to a factory in Germany. Then
she had worked her way to a displaced persons' camp in Austria,
and had later been moved to Italy. The man had been caught up
in the Russian advance over Poland from the East, and taken to
work in Siberia. He had been allowed to leave the USSR through
Afghanistan and made his way to India. From there he went to
a displaced persons' camp in Mozambique. It is incredible that
the IRO was able to find the couple and their son, reunite them,
and send them off to a new life in Canada together.

People are not statistics. Of course in one sense they are
thankful to be alive and ready to put their hand to anything.

But each is an individual, sometimes with a skill or vocation which is a part of them. It is heartwarming to read how some-times—often—the IRO succeeded in fitting square pegs into square holes—Canadian industry recruiting skilled engineers, a Hungarian musician conducting an orchestra in Bogota, a Russian microbiologist countering soil-erosion in Ethiopia, a Czech doctor going as medical officer on a scientific expedition. Yet these were relatively easy to fit in, and we must applaud those governments who took in people in need of institutional care—100 blind in Norway, 150 tubercular with their depend-ents in Sweden, 980 aged in France, 600 mental sufferers in UK, 1500 in need of various forms of care in the USA (including Mrs. Pauline Wilsdorf who celebrated her hundredth birthday). Nations can behave with altruism.

The IRO's life was extended more than once, not least through the representations of voluntary bodies, such as the United Nations Association. In 1952 it was wound up, having been replaced by a High Commissioner for Refugees. There remained an enormous task. In the mid-1950s there were thought to be about 70,000,000 refugees, about 1 in 30 of the world's people. Dr. G. J. van Heuven Goedhart, the first High Com-missioner, who sadly died young in 1956, had only the previous year received the Nobel Peace Prize on behalf of his Office.

Meantime a separate UN organization, UNRWA (Relief and Works Agency) has been called to meet the intransigent problems of Palestinian refugees who have been pawns in the game of Near Eastern politics, unable or unwilling to return to their former homes in Israel, and not assimilated by the States round about who wish to maintain the claim on their original homeland. It has been in operation for thirty-five years, and cares for about two million people. It provides homes, and services for those homes. It provides food for those in need, though most refugee families have been encouraged to become self-supporting. It provides health care with such success that there has never been a serious epidemic of communicable disease; indeed, during a cholera outbreak in the Near East, the epidemic was kept from spreading through the camps more successfully than among the general population. Schooling is provided for 330,000 school children in conditions as near normalcy as possible: further training is given to over 5000 students. UNRWA is actually the largest UN agency in terms of staff, and, after national governments, is the largest employer in the Near East, the vast majority of the 17,000 posts being held by local recruits.

Bernard Mossaz, the Chief of the Relief Services Division, said a year or two ago: 'The Palestine question may be an old story, but unfortunately none of the problems of the Palestine refugees are being solved. This is not recognised well enough by the international community. Right or wrong (and I hope I am wrong), the rest of the world does not seem to realise that the problem is very acute and that our existence is unfortunately still necessary, as are the means to support us.' (Those means have come predominantly from USA, EEC, Japan, Sweden, UK and 70 other governments including those in the area of operations.) Since then, the tragic events in the Lebanon have reinforced the need, and created further emergencies. It must be remembered that, whether or not guerrilla groups have been operating from the refugee camps, the vast majority of the refugees are ordinary people wanting desperately to live normal lives.

And the rest of the world's people who do not realize that the problem is very acute, do not appreciate what has been achieved over a third of a century for human beings, men, women and children, in need.

Neither does the wider challenge go away. Between 1970 and 1980, the UN High Commissioner's annual budget grew from $8.3m to almost $500m. Refugees currently in the care of the High Commissioner (remember that this does not include the Palestinians) number as follows, the country being the one in which they have taken refuge:

Pakistan	2,900,000
Iran	1,800,000
USA	1,000,000
Somalia	700,000
Sudan	690,000

Canada	353,000
Australia	317,000
Zaire	303,500
Burundi	256,300
Algeria	167,000
France	161,200
Mexico	160,000
UK	140,000
Uganda	133,000
Thailand	133,000
Zambia	103,000
Angola	96,200
Guatemala	70,000

and smaller numbers elsewhere. These figures do not of course include those who have been successfully assimilated. But assimilation becomes more difficult, and governments have become less generous and more restrictive, especially with the growth in unemployment.

Voluntary repatriation remains the most desirable solution. It depends of course on changes in the political climate. The UNHCR and his staff are always on the lookout for this solution. Two recent examples include the return of 250,000 to Zimbabwe in 1981 and of 150,000 to Chad in 1981. An independent Namibia would see a similar emptying of the camps.

Local integration has been another solution. Perhaps the most remarkable has been the integration of 260,000 Vietnamese in China in state farms and fishing, with co-operation between the Chinese government and the international community. In Tanzania, the Sudan and Zaire, there has been similar integration in rural settlements. In Pakistan there are major problems since the land is too poor to support an additional three million, but the World Bank has designed a $20m infrastructure improvement project which is refugee-labour-intensive and will also be of help to the local community (as refugee services often are). The industrialized countries have resettled about a million refugees from SE Asia. If it is not always easy for the citizens of the host country we should not forget that the refugees have to learn a new language, and cope with an unfamiliar culture, traditions and values.

Immense problems remain, not least in SE Asia. One journalist wrote, 'In Indo-China the wars end, one after another, but ten years later the people are still there, the last to hang on, until others come along, with their smiles, their miseries, their despair. The people tossed to and fro by war, on the frontier between Thailand and Kampuchea, and the boat people, are the forgotten ones in a story which one so much wants to see finished that one wipes the most recent developments from one's mind.'

Two recent developments in UNHCR policy shows something of the problems. The Boat People have suffered immeasurably from pirate attacks off the coast of Thailand. The High Commissioner has worked in close cooperation with the Thai Government in an anti-piracy programme. This has reduced the incidence of piracy by 20%, an improvement but not sufficient. Further measures are in hand; one difficulty is the ignorance over the identity of the pirates.

Another development has been the institution of mobile 'roving officers' on the frontier between Honduras and El Salvador. This enables refugees to be promptly rescued and gives them protection and security from the moment of crossing the frontier. One effect has been that the refugees have crossed the frontier specifically where the roving officers are positioned, sometimes after a fifteen-days' route march. It was not unusual for the roving officers to approach a border post with the UN flag, and suddenly to see 100 or even 250 people emerge.

One thing the High Commissioner must not do is 'get embroiled in the political fray'. It might win him praise in some quarters, but, in the long run, many doors would be closed to him, and he would be hindered in carrying out his essentially humanitarian function of protecting the right of refugees, and finding a durable solution for each individual. He will, and does, protest against governments if refugees' rights are threatened. But, however true it is that the reason for refugees lies in the political order or disorder, and however desirable it is for the problem of refugees to be tackled at the root, that is not the High Commissioner's task.

That task has been faithfully carried out. As one recent High Commissioner has said, 'When in so many fields, so much international effort achieves so little, we can point to 25 million refugees who have passed through our books on their way to a new life.'

12 Human Rights

Human rights form a characteristic concern of our time. They are identified, upheld and infringed. But once they are identified and upheld, they cannot be infringed with total impunity.

Article 1 of the UN Charter declares that one of the basic aims of the UN is to achieve international cooperation in promoting and encouraging respect for human rights and fundamental freedoms for all without distinction as to race, sex, language or religion. On 26 June 1945, the President of the United States said with relation to the Charter: 'Under this document we have good reason to expect an international bill of rights acceptable to all the nations involved. That bill of rights will be as much a part of international life as our own Bill of Rights is a part of our own Constitution. The Charter is dedicated to the achievement and observance of human rights and fundamental freedoms. Unless we can attain these objectives for all men and women everywhere without regard to race, language, or religion—we cannot have permanent peace and security in the world.'

The matter was referred to the Economic and Social Council, who on 16 February 1946 determined to establish a commission whose chief sphere of action should be human rights. It is almost unbelievable that within less than three years, in such a highly contentious field, the Universal Declaration of Human Rights should be approved by the UN General Assembly without opposition. The date, 10 December, has thereafter been celebrated as Human Rights Day.

What emerged has many roots. The first two articles are fundamental:

1. All human beings are born free and equal in dignity and rights. They are endowed with reason and conscience and should act towards one another in a spirit of brotherhood.

2. Everyone is entitled to all the rights and freedoms set forth
   in this Declaration, without distinction of any kind, such as
   race, colour, sex, language, religion, political or other opinion,
   national or social origin, property, birth or other status.

   Furthermore, no distinction shall be made on the basis of the
   political, jurisdictional or international status of the country or
   territory to which a person belongs, whether this territory be an
   independent, Trust or Non-Self-Governing territory.

This is indebted to the Christian tradition, both the New Tes-
tament and the Reformation, to the Enlightenment, Rousseau,
Locke, Paine and Kant, and to the two great revolutions in the
United States and France.

Legal aspects of the Declaration can be traced to Deuter-
onomy, Plato, Magna Carta and English Common Law. The
principles of freedom of movement and the right to nationality
were based on Woodrow Wilson's Fourteen Points and the
League of Nations. Emphasis on the family was based on
Judaism and China. Freedom of thought and utterance has its
classic expressions in Socrates, Milton, Mill and the Declaration
of Independence. The clauses relating to government come from
Magna Carta, the Declaration of Independence and the French
and Russian Revolutions. The articles relating to social security
and the standard of living owe something to Plato, More's Utopia,
Owen, Bismarck, Marx, Lloyd George, Roosevelt and Attlee.
The emphasis on education is found in Plato and Aristotle,
the Protestant Reformers, the Prussian reforms of 1794. The
stress on duties comes from Plato, Hobbes, Engels, and the
Soviet Union.

It was no small achievement that a document was agreed
nem. con. when one reflects on the vastness of some of the
divergences. For example, Mrs. Roosevelt and the Americans
took an individualistic stance and maintained the rights of the
individual against the world, whereas the Soviet Union was by
no means alone in affirming that the individual is free so long
and only so long as their freedom does not hamper the workings
of society. Or again, Mrs. Roosevelt wanted the right of owning
private property written into the Declaration. This was obviously
alien to the thinking of the Soviet delegate, Prof. Alexis Pavlov.

But it was the delegate from Haiti who said that this was alto-
gether too individualistic, and needed some such clause as 'that
the right should be used in the interest of the general welfare,'
and the delegate from Panama who pointed out that property is
not everywhere recognized, and it could be considered as a right
only subject to the general laws of any country.

Indeed there was no agreement over the basis of human
rights. One group held that they are a part of natural law, *ius
naturale*. A second group believed them to be part of the law of
God, *ius divinum*. A third group preferred not to use this language
but held nonetheless that human rights are universal and eternal.
A fourth group asserted that human rights are the state or stage
which human beings reach in their struggle for progress and are
constituted by the conquests achieved.

The Declaration was called Universal, and intended as such,
but the whole formulation was dominated by the history of
Europe and North America. Forty years later it might have
been somewhat different.

The great influx of newly independent countries into the UN
has properly affected the outlook, emphasis and priorities within
the field of human rights as elsewhere. The particular concerns
have been the right of political self-determination, the elimination
of all forms of racial discrimination, and the need for international
action to combat hunger, disease and illiteracy. These rights are
all implicit in the Universal Declaration, but they did not in the
early days have the same level of priority.

It will be at once noted that the problem, as so often,
is one of translating principles into action. Self-determination
seems obvious in the face of colonial régimes, but it creates
practical problems when the nation concerned is simply too
small and too resourceless to be viable as an independent state
in the modern world. Further, there are problems about the
self-determination of minorities, especially when those minorities
have sub-minorities within them. The Nigerian civil war of the
late 1960s was not so much about the right of the Igbos to self-
determination, but about their non-right to drag out with them
forcibly the people of the Rivers in whose territory the major
oil resources had been discovered. The situation in Northern

Ireland is almost an inversion of this. Here a portion of the island is politically distinct from the south. In it a privileged Protestant majority has governed an underprivileged Catholic minority. But if the self-determination of the minority took the north into unity with the south, the majority would now become the minority. These problems of the self-determination of parts of integral states are with us all over the world; witness the Punjabis of India or the Tamils of Sri Lanka, to cite two examples. Even the Scots and Welsh in Britain!

With regard to the elimination of racial discrimination and the fight against hunger, disease and illiteracy, the real problem is securing international action. The main offender against the former is South Africa, and it has been easy enough to secure unanimous condemnation of her policies, but less easy to persuade the powerful nations with strong interests in that country to accept the cost of common international action which might achieve the necessary changes, particularly as the West sees South Africa as a partner in combatting communism. So too, the fight against hunger, disease and illiteracy depends in the end upon the 'haves' being willing to place more of their resources at the service of the 'have-nots'. As we have seen, in the end this is enlightened self-interest, but few have acted upon it.

Fresh voices have not been solely concerned with racial and economic discrimination. Two major concerns which have reared their head since 1948 have been the rights of the child and the status of women.

Mark Twain, in a well-known after-dinner toast to the Babies, pointed out that we have not all been Presidents or international sportsmen, but we have all been babies.

The Declaration of the Rights of the Child, adopted by the General Assembly in 1959, elaborates upon article 25 of the Universal Declaration, and insists that all children shall be given opportunities and facilities by law and other means to enable them to develop physically, mentally, morally, spiritually, and socially, in a healthy and normal manner and in conditions of freedom and dignity. These include a name and nationality; education which shall be free and compulsory, at least in the elementary stages;

adequate nutrition, housing, recreation and medical services; protection against neglect, cruelty and exploitation.

Equal rights of men and women is a cardinal principle of the UN Charter, but women do not enjoy them over much of the world. The General Assembly in 1946 urged the implementation of this principle, and the Commission on the Status of Women began its work in the same year. What the Commission has achieved across the years is a detailed examination worldwide of all manner of issues affecting women—the dissolution of marriage, tax legislation, inheritance laws, the nationality of married women, access to education, pension rights, family planning and much else. In 1967 the General Assembly adopted a Declaration on the Elimination of Discrimination Against Women. A report to the Secretary-General at much the same time proposed a programme

   (a) To promote the universal recognition of the dignity and worth of the human person and of the equal rights of men and women in accordance with the Charter of the United Nations and the Universal Declaration of Human Rights;

   (b) to enable women to participate fully in the development of society in order that society may benefit from the contribution of all its members;

   (c) to stimulate an awareness among both men and women of women's full potential and of the importance of their contribution to the development of society.

The promotion of human rights is carried out by special studies, fellowships, scholarships and seminars, the provision of advisory services, not least to governments about necessary legislative changes; and periodic reports. What this does is to raise the threshold of awareness, and the pressure of public opinion.

In addition, over the eighteen years which followed the passing of the Universal Declaration, two International Covenants were prepared, one on Civil and Political Rights and the other on Economic, Social and Cultural Rights, both passing the General Assembly in 1966 by over 100 votes to 0. These spell out obligations rather than principles. There are however three major problems about them. First, even though they are intended to deal with legal obligations, some, such as freedom of thought, are almost impossible to incorporate legally. Secondly, some of the rights within the Covenants are hedged round with limitations and restrictions. This may become almost meaningless. For instance the provision that the rights shall not be subject to any restrictions except those which are specified by law may not be of much help. What if the law be oppressive—or merely an ass! So, thirdly, it was perhaps a mistake to draw up such extensive and comprehensive covenants. The difficulty is that a state may become a party out of general intent, but specific implementation may be long delayed—or a state may refrain from becoming a party to the whole covenant because of reservations over a particular clause. During the period of the League, Albert Thomas, the dynamic Director of the ILO, hawked individual conventions, each incorporating a particular point of labour or industrial legislation, round the world until the nations were one by one shamed into incorporating that specific change of law.

However the Covenants have been accepted by something like one third of the nations, and they do include the obligation to submit regular reports on their work to protect human rights. The Civil and Political Covenant also includes a system of nation-to-nation complaints, and an Optional Protocol, whereby it is binding on those nations who have signed this (only a third of those signing the covenant) that an individual citizen may complain to the Human Rights Committee over any alleged infringement. This is a major breakthrough in international law.

It should be remembered also that the UN can work through regional organizations, and the first convention concluded between the member states of the Council of Europe was in fact the European Convention for the Protection of Human Rights and Fundamental Freedoms, signed in Rome on 4 November 1950. This was based on the Universal Declaration, but tauter and more precise. The European Commission for Human Rights receives complaints, and will seek a private settlement. If this is not possible the matter is referred to the Court of Human Rights (established in 1958), provided that the government involved has accepted the jurisdiction. Decisions of the Court are binding. One interesting judgement was given in April 1978 to the effect that birching on the Isle of Man should be brought to an end, being a degrading practice. Plainly, decisions such as this have wider implications both for legislation and for practice. Similarly the Inter-American Commission on Human Rights has had some influence, and there has been talk on an African Commission.

Human Rights matter. Keith Suter of the Australian UNA in an excellent pamphlet *Protecting Human Rights* has scotched some cynical criticisms:

(a) 'There are more human rights violations now than ever before.' There are more human rights, and more people to violate them! But there are no possible scientific grounds for such an assertion. For the first time we are beginning to account for violations.

(b) 'Attitudes don't change.' This is simply untrue. There are improvements in the status of women. There is far more criticism of racist humour than even thirty years ago.

(c) 'Governments aren't interested in human rights, only in keeping in power.' Cynical, but governments may develop an interest in human rights in order to keep in power.

(d) 'There is nothing for the individual to do to protect human rights.' Amnesty International alone has shown this to be untrue.

The balance of achievement and ongoing need can be illustrated from the year 1978—it would be possible to draw up a similar estimate at almost any time. At that time in Singapore there was arbitrary arrest, detention without trial, and torture; three men had been held for seventeen years without trial. In Saudi Arabia there were summary trials and executions. In Rhodesia there were 5000 unconvicted detainees. In Guatemala journalists were abducted. In USSR there was a major crackdown on dissenters. In Yugoslavia a freethinking journalist was placed in a psychiatric hospital. In Northern Ireland the Bennett Report confirmed the maltreatment of detainees. In Taiwan there were 101 arrests after a demonstration for human rights. In Mozambique 7500 Jehovah's Witnesses were being compulsorily reeducated. In Namibia South African troops beat people with rifle butts. Malawi passed detention laws for political purposes. In Argentina there was abduction and systematic torture; 15,000 people were reported missing. In the Dominican Republic Julio de Peña Valdez, a Trade Union leader, was kept naked in an underground cell.

On the other hand, through the force of world public opinion, Sr. Peña was released. There was a general amnesty in Iraq including Kurds, Christians and Freemasons. In Israel, Mayor Bassan Shal'a of Nablus was released from detention and threatened deportation. Indonesia released all prisoners who were untried or uncharged. In Nigeria the government abolished the military special tribunals and suspended death sentences. In Tanzania the Zanzibar Treason Trial prisoners were released.

So the fight for a free and just society is never won finally. Vigilance is always needed. But it is not without its victories.

On 26 October 1982 Javier Perez de Cuellar, the UN Secretary-General, made an important speech in New York in the course of which he stressed the inextricable relationship between human rights and world peace. He faced the question that high principles were enunciated and then ignored, and gave a two-fold answer:

First, the concept of specific human rights is not one which developed simultaneously and identically in all parts of the world. It is only possible to hold Governments to certain standards if these standards are the same for all—large and small—and if they have been concurred in and understood. In a sense, the codification by the international community of human rights amounts to the establishment of a global conscience when none, in all of history, has existed before. As individuals we do not always follow the dictates of our conscience. Neither do nations, but there can be no credible excuse now that human rights are violated because universal standards do not exist.

The existence of these standards is important for a second reason. In many areas of the world, people have yet to develop a full understanding of the rights to which they are entitled as human beings. People cannot claim respect of, or act in the defence of, human rights unless they know what these rights are. That is why, within the United Nations human rights programme, importance has been attached to the dissemination of basic international human rights instruments in as many languages as possible on a world-wide basis.

I believe there is presently a wider concern with human rights issues—a greater sensitivity to human rights violations—than ever before. Yet, even so, people continue to be persecuted, imprisoned and, in some cases, executed, without due process of law. The protection of human rights to which most nations are committed requires broad, continuing efforts on the part of private citizens, of

111

Governments and non-governmental organizations and, not least, by the United Nations.

Let me emphasise, in this connection, that concern for the protection of basic human rights legitimately transcends national boundaries. One of the purposes of the United Nations is to achieve international co-operation in promoting respect for human rights and for fundamental freedoms for all. The Universal Declaration of Human Rights states that 'no distinction shall be made on the basis of the political, jurisdictional or international status of the country or territory to which a person belongs.'

This principle now finds specific reflection in the human rights activities of the United Nations. The Human Rights Commission is authorised to examine information relevant to gross violations of human rights and fundamental freedoms and to make a thorough study of situations which reveal a consistent pattern of violation of human rights. The Human Rights Committee hears periodic reports form the States which have so far ratified the International Covenant on Civil and Political Rights. Under the Optional Protocol to this Covenant, individuals residing in the countries which have ratified it can lodge complaints with the Secretary-General relative to violations of rights guaranteed under the Covenant. When violations of human rights are confirmed the only means available to the United Nations to bring about compliance with the Covenant is the force of publicity and international censure. But this force can be considerable.

What I would like to emphasise is that there are functioning instrumentalities in the United Nations which operate on the principle that respect for human rights is the legitimate concern of the United Nations. This principle is not subject to serious question. The results as we know are far from satisfactory—but they are greater than in the past. In my first press conference after becoming Secretary-General I said that I intend to play an active role within the limits of my functions as laid down in the Charter with the view to seeing to it that human rights are respected by everyone, whether it be in the North, South, East or West. This remains my intent and I have made structural changes in the Organization which I hope will further this goal. But the most essential requirements are for Governments to follow in practice the standards which they have defined and accepted in principle and for people as individuals and as groups to respect the human person—every human life.

As in the case of human rights, the international community has established in the Charter of the United Nations a standard for the conduct of international relations. I believe it is essential that the nations of the world again accept the Charter as the guide and standard of international conduct it was intended to be. They must use and support the means which the Charter provides for the preservation of peace. This I would suggest is the urgent appeal that must be made to the human conscience in our time.

The achievement of the past forty years has been great. 1948 seems like another world. The right to self-government has been realized all through the former colonial empires. Improvements in working conditions have taken place and, despite the prevalence of unemployment, no-one is happy about it or regards a pool of unemployed as a necessary or proper incentive to work. The principle of social security is widely accepted. Governments who practise human rights violations—and there remain many who do—no longer boast about it, and dislike being exposed. Voluntary organizations such as Amnesty International keep public opinion alerted. More and more people are aware of their rights.

The major role in all this has fallen to the UN. The Universal Declaration of Human Rights sparked off modern concerns in this field. The General Assembly, the Human Rights Commission and many of the organs of the UN provide forums where violations can be challenged. If there is much still to do, much has been done, and Keith Suter has looked beyond the proper and necessary attempt to remedy current abuses to a more ultimate goal when he writes: 'The creation of a genuine international community which transcends national frontiers, will only come about through the creation of unity—though not necessarily uniformity—in terms of cultures and values. By protecting human rights, the UN is simultaneously working at the foundations of what will be a genuine international community of people.'

13 The Present and the Future

The UN has changed greatly since its inception, and some nations have failed to come to terms with that change. In the early days it was dominated by the United States and Western Europe. The USSR were there of course, except for a short period of self-induced absence which they came to regret. They used the veto to protect their own interests, used it vigorously and often: Ambassador Malik was popularly known as 'Mr. Veto'.

The increasing representation of the newly independent nations of the Third World has changed the face of the UN. Remember that, apart from the veto, in the UN every sovereign state is equal. But before we fulminate too brightly about democracy it is well to recall that the South (if we include India and China) is where the people are. The present balance does not represent 'one person one vote', but we of Western Europe would be fairly insignificant if we changed to that principle. Those who grumble at the UN as a 'Third World Club' are sometimes regretting the lost power of colonial imperialism, and sometimes wanting the UN to reflect more closely the actualities of economic and military power. But economic and military power are already actualities, and it is better if they are not reflected in the UN, which can then form a check on them, however modest, in the interests of the rest of the world. At the same time the rest of the world has no right to expect the economically powerful to contribute to excess to an organ where they have only a minority representation. There is a delicate balance to hold.

If the former dominant powers are dissatisfied with the strong Third World presence in the UN, it is also true that the Third World countries are dissatisfied with the continued dominance of those powers. This is accentuated by a generation gap. The delegates from Western Europe and the USA—and the USSR—tend to be appreciably older than the younger delegates from the newer countries, some of whom were not born in 1945 and in the words of Davidson Nicol of Sierra Leone 'are completely unimpressed by the former historical dominance of Europe and the United States and have only a passing acquaintance with the Second World War and the Holocaust'. They see the economic organs of the UN dominated by the financial interests of the North. They resent bitterly some occasions when Britain, France and the USA have used the veto, seeing these vetoes as springing from neo-colonialist and even racist attitudes.

It is in fact notable that, whereas in the early days the USSR used the veto frequently, today the USSR seldom has occasion to do so, and the USA is the predominant user of the veto. It is important to see that few, very few, of the younger nations are aligned with the USSR in the world power struggle. They are genuinely non-aligned. For this reason we ought to be listening to their voices.

The problem is that the Great Powers expect the UN to subserve their interests. The USA and the USSR tend to act bilaterally; an appalling example was the Yom Kippur War of 1973 when the rest of the world had to wait for the USA and USSR to determine when the fighting should stop, and the UN was used as a rubber stamp not as the instrument of peacemaking.

The USA wants the UN to be its ally against communism and the USSR, is disappointed when the Third World does not toe its line, and sometimes becomes petulant. When Britain and France did not agree to bring affairs in Poland to the Security Council (being internal to Poland), Senator Moynihan proposed that the US should do so, and that, if Britain and France did not support them, should downgrade its representation at the UN from an Ambassador to a Third Secretary!

Britain at the Falklands Islands crisis acted somewhat ambivalently. Let it be clear that the aggression by the Argentine was a grave offence against international law, and that under international law Britain had a right of self-defence. The issue was in fact taken to the Security Council and the Argentine invasion was condemned. The Argentine had in fact expected the Third World to support them in cocking a snook at the former colonial power. They did nothing of the kind. They condemned the aggression and the breach of international law. But now two things happened. First Britain had a choice between asking the Security Council to act and going it alone. We chose to go it alone and in so doing changed the matter from, 'This is a grave breach of international law' to 'You can't push us around.' An opportunity was missed, and the lesson taught was not, 'Don't commit acts of aggression' but, 'Don't take on someone bigger than yourself who will hit back.' At the same time Britain ignored the Security Council resolution calling for military disengagement. It is not until the nations comprising the UN put the UN first in their foreign policy, and do not use it as a convenience, last resort, or adjunct to an independent foreign policy, that the UN can become fully effective. For (it cannot be said too often) the UN is the nations comprising it.

Can we ever expect this? Yes. People can behave unselfishly; witness the foodparcels sent to Germany in 1946 when Britain was enduring shortages but Germany was starving, or the tremendous response to the media revelation of starving children in Ethiopia. Nations are made up of people, and if the people want to act unselfishly, the nation can and should do so.

But in the long run, it is a matter of enlightened self-interest. The Russians play the system as hard as anyone else. But they play it rigidly according to the rules, though they will push those rules hard. In the end they know that it is in their interests to have an ordered and cooperating world within limits which all agree. And so it is. Davidson Nicol in *The Cambridge Review* (22.10.82) wrote, 'The United Nations will have failed if it agrees to be only the instrument of world power or bloc. It must always first consider how that power aligns itself with the primary functions and goals of international peace and security demanded by the United Nations Charter.' 'Sooner or later,' wrote Brian Urquhart, an Under Secretary-General, 'the human community will be faced with a situation where world peace—and perhaps survival—will depend on the governments concerned in an acute crisis giving

117

priority to the general international good rather than to specific national interests.'

The fact is that many people do not like the UN because they do not like the world as it is today. But it is the only world we have. Margaret Fuller was once heard to say, 'I accept the universe,' on which Coleridge commented, 'By God, she'd better!' In the world we have, the UN is the best protection against things falling right apart.

No doubt more can be done. Let us take security. The British UNA in 1983 submitted an important paper to the World Federation of UNAs on 'Strengthening the Security Role of the UN'. They say, 'Practical progress in this field depends primarily on the positive attitude of UN Member States,' just as we have already said. They make five proposals:

1. The Security Council should instruct the Secretary-General to bring threatening situations to them as early as possible, and that he should have a group of diplomatic, military and economic experts available for areas of potential conflict.

2. He should report annually to the Foreign Ministers of the Member States of the Security Council on the world situation.

3. Methods of strengthening arbitration procedures should be considered, perhaps with a treaty whereby Member States undertake to go to arbitration in a dispute.

4. Peacekeeping forces should be given the capability of fulfilling their mandate.

5. The Palme Commission's proposals for extending peacekeeping towards peace-enforcement should be seriously considered.

These are modest enough proposals. Their acceptance, and the consequent increase of effectiveness in the UN, depends not on the UN but on the nations composing it. Us among them.

Or consider what we have already said about giving peace a positive content. This depends on the 'haves' giving more aid to the 'have-nots'. This, as we have shown, is in everyone's interest. It depends upon achieving the 0.7% of GNP asked for aid. It depends upon stabilizing the prices of primary commodities. It depends upon giving the Third World a more effective voice in the international economic structures. The UN has all the machinery for making a happier, healthier, juster world. It is the nations which lack the will. We among them.

Instead, we grumble as if the UN were a needless extravagance. We must maintain our sense of proportion. The UN produces a lot of paper. It has to do so. The annual agenda of the Assembly may amount to 130 items, with supporting documents, which have to be circulated in six languages. It produces research papers, often dull to plough through, but vitally important, and is a major source for global statistics, all again in six languages. But the total amount of paper used by the UN in a year is less than the New York Times uses for one single Sunday edition. The whole staff of the UN system is 44,000, to serve over 150 nations, about the same number as the civil servants in Alberta. Again there are sometimes complaints about the expense of the UN and its agencies, like the charges recently levelled at Unesco. The careful stewardship of money is always appropriate. Still the UN's regular budget is smaller than that of the New York City Police Department. The combined budgets of the whole UN family come to less than that of the State of Louisiana (with its 4,000,000 inhabitants). It is one-twentieth the federal budget of Canada with 0.5% of world's people. The world expenditure on arms over one year would pay for the whole UN system for well over a century. How much are we prepared to spend on peace? Give peace a chance.

Many people have the most limited notion of what the UN does. A list of some major UN conferences—additional of course to the normal meetings of the UN and its agencies—in 1983 is not without interest.

1 March—8 April (Vienna) UN Conference on Succession of States in respect of State Property, Archives and Debts. — Major issues of international law.

23–29 April (Paris) International Conference in Support of the Struggle of the Namibian People for Independence. — A UN plan for Namibia was drawn up in 1976 and 1978.

6–30 June (Belgrade) Sixth Session of UNCTAD. — To review world development and its impact on the trade and development of developing countries.

10 – 11 June (Geneva) International Conference of Trades Unions on Sanctions and Other Actions against the Apartheid Regime in South Africa

1 – 12 August (Geneva) Second World Conference to Combat Racism and Racial Discrimination

16 – 27 August (Paris) International Conference on the Question of Palestine

29 August—7 September (Geneva) UN Conference for the Promotion of International Cooperation in the Peaceful Use of Nuclear Energy

But these are only a few meetings. Even more telling is the schedule of meetings over a couple of months. The months happen to be February and March 1985, but they are chosen at random.

FEBRUARY

4 – 8 (IMO) Sub-Committee on Fire Protection, 30th session (London)

4 – 9 (ESCAP/WMO) Meeting on the Establishment of a Cyclone Council for the South Pacific (Port Vila, Vanuatu)

4 – 13 (UN) Advisory Committee on Science and Technology for Development, 5th session (New York)

4 Feb—15 March (UN) Commission on Human Rights, 41st session (New York)

5 – 8 (UN) Economic and Social Council, organizational session (New York)

7 (UN) Commission on Narcotic Drugs – Sub-Commission on Illicit Drug Traffic and related Matters in the Near and Middle East (Vienna)

8 (UN) Commission on Narcotic Drugs—Steering Committee (organizational meeting) (Vienna)

11 – 14 (ECE) Group of Rapporteurs on Pollution and Energy, 11th session (Geneva)

11 – 15 (ECE) Working Party on Electronic Data Processing, 19th session (Geneva)

11–15 (IMO) Sub-Committee on Containers and Cargoes, 26th session (London)

11–15 (UN) High-level Intergovernmental Meeting on Agro-Industry Development (Brasilia)

11–20 (UN) Commission on Narcotic Drugs, 31st session (Vienna)

11–22 (UN) Committee on the Peaceful Uses of Outer Space—Scientific and Technical Sub-Committee, 22nd session (New York)

11 Feb—1 March (ILO) 229th session of the Governing Body and its Committees (Geneva)

12–16 (Unesco) Executive Board. Extraordinary Session (to examine the consequences of the withdrawal of the United States) (Paris)

18–22 (ECE) Senior Economic Advisers to ECE Governments (Geneva)

18–22 (UNCTAD) Committee on Invisibles and Financing related to Trade, 11th session. 2nd part (Geneva)

18–27 (UN) Commission for Social Development, 29th session (Vienna)

18 Feb—8 March (UNCTAD) UN Cocoa Conference 1984. 3rd part (Geneva)

19–22 (FAO) Commission on Fertilizers, 9th session (Rome)

19–22 (IAEA) Board of Governors (Vienna)

19–22 (UNDP) Governing Council, organizational and special meeting (New York)

19–28 (UN) Population Commission, 23rd session (New York)

19 Feb—1 March (UN) Third Regional Cartographic Conference for the Americas (New York)

19—8 March (UN) Group of Experts on the Reduction of Military Budgets (New York)

21–22 (UN) Inter-Agency Meeting on Co-ordination in Matters of International Drug Abuse (Vienna)

25 (UN) Investments Committee (New York)

25–26 (UN) Committee for the UN Population Award (New York)

25–28 (UN) Latin American and Caribbean Regional Seminar for the International Year of Peace (New York)

121

25 – 28 (WHO) Working Group on Crisis Intervention and Psychiatric Emergency Services in Europe (Vienna)

25 Feb—1 March (FAO/WHO) 5th Seminar on Trypanosomiasis (Harare)

25 Feb—1 March (IMO) Sub-Committee on Stability and Load Lines and on Fishing Vessels Safety, 30th session (London)

25 Feb—6 March (UN) Statistical Commission, 23rd session (New York)

25 Feb—8 March (UNCTAD) Committee on Invisibles and Financing related to Trade, 11th session, 2nd part. (Geneva)

25 Feb—15 March (UNCTAD) UN Conference on an International Code of Conduct on the Transfer of Technology (Geneva)

25 Feb—29 March (ICAO) Council, 114th session (Montreal)

26 Feb—5 March (WMO) 6th session of the Joint Scientific Committee (London)

28 Feb—1 March (UN) Ad Hoc Committee on the Preparations for the Public Hearings on the Activities of Transnational Corporations in South Africa and Namibia (New York)

MARCH

1 (UN) Pledging Conference for the International Year of Peace (New York)

4 – 6 (UN) Asian and Pacific Regional Seminar to Commemorate the 25th Anniversary of the Adoption of the Declaration of the Granting of Independence to Colonial Countries and Peoples (Port Moresby)

4 – 8 (FAO/IAEA) International Symposium on Food Irradiation Processing (Washington DC)

4 – 13 (UN) Commission on the Status of Women acting as the Preparatory Body for the Conference to Review and Appraise the Achievements of the UN Decade for Women, 3rd session (Vienna)

4 – 15 (UN) Group of Governmental Experts to carry out a Comprehensive Study of the Naval Forces and Naval Arms Race, Naval Forces and Naval Arms Systems, 3rd session (New York)

4 – 22 (UN) Committee on the Elimination of Racial Discrimination, 31st session (New York)

4 – 29 (UN) Special Committee on the Charter of the UN and the Strengthening of the Role of the Organization (New York)

5 – 8 (ECE) Senior Advisers to ECE Governments on Environmental Problems, 13th session (Geneva)

6 – 8 (UN) Preparatory Commission for the International Sea-bed Authority and for the International Tribunal for the law of the Sea—Group of 77 (Kingston)

11 – 14 (ECE/INSTRAW) Meeting on Statistics and Indicators on the Role and Situation of Women (Geneva)

11 – 15 (ECE) Committee on Agricultural Problems, 36th Session (Geneva)

11 – 15 (FAO) Commission on Plant Genetic Resources, 1st session (Rome)

11 – 22 (UN) Committee on Non-Governemental Organizations (New York)

11 – 22 (UN) Intergovernmental Working Group of Experts on International Standards of Accounting and Reporting, 3rd session (New York)

11 – 29 (UN) International Civil Service Commission, 21st session (London)

11 March—4 April (UN) Preparatory Commission for the International Sea-bed Authority and for the International Tribunal for the Law of the Sea, 3rd session (Kingston)

15 – 16 (ECE) Steering Committee forthe Inter-Country Project on International Cooperative Research on Low-Calorie Solid Fuels Technology, 1st meeting (Geneva)

18 – 22 (UN) Conference of Plenipotentiaries on the Protection of the Ozone Layer (Vienna)

18 – 22 (UN) Human Rights Committee—Working Group on Communications (New York)

18 – 27 (FAO) Committee on Agriculture, 8th session (Rome)

18 – 29 (UNCTAD) Trade and Development Board, 30th session (Geneva)

18 March—4 April (UN) Committee on the Peaceful Uses of Outer Space—Legal Sub-Committee, 24th session (New York)

19–29 (ESCAP) Economic and Social Commission for Asia and the Pacific, 41st Session (Bangkok)

20–22 (ECE) Working Party on Air Pollution Problems, 14th session (Geneva)

21 (UN) Special Committee against Apartheid—Special Meeting in Observance of the International Day for the Elimination of Racial Discrimination (New York)

21–22 (ECE) Preparatory meeting for the Symposium on Status and Prospects of New and Renewable Sources of Energy in the ECE Region (Geneva)

25–27 (ECE) 6th Seminar on East-West Trade Promotion, Marketing and Business Contacts (Geneva)

25–29 (ECE) Group of Rapporteurs on the Construction and Operation of the Trans-European North/South Motorway Project

25–29 (IMO) Legal Committee, 54th session (London)

25–29 (UN) Consultative Committee on the Voluntary Fund for the UN Decade for Women (New York)

25 March—1 April (FAO) Codex Committee on Pesticide Residues, 17th Session (The Hague)

25 March—4 April (UN) Ad Hoc Committee on the Indian Ocean (New York)

25 March—4 April (UN) Group of Governmental Experts on International Co–operation to Avert New Flows of Refugees, 5th session (New York)

25 March—12 April (UN) Ad Hoc Intergovernmental Committee of the Whole to Review the Implementation of the Charter of Economic Rights and Duties of States (New York)

25 March—12 April (UN) Human Rights Committee, 24th session (New York)

25–28 (UN) Western Asian Regional Expert Group Preparatory Meeting for the UN Conference for the Promotion of International Co-operation in the Peaceful Uses of Nuclear Energy (Baghdad)

25–29 (UN) Seminar of Council for Namibia (Abidjan, Ivory Coast)

25 March—3 April (UN) Advisory Committee for the International Youth Year (Vienna)

124

There, over two months, are more than eighty meetings. At every one, representatives of different nations from all over the world were meeting peaceably in constructive discussion. To read the popular press one might think that the UN is all wars and rumours of wars. The UN is about working together for the things that make for peace. Many of these themes—cyclones, the illicit drug traffic, pollution, fertilizers, trypanosomiasis, plant genetic resources, the protection of the ozone layer, pesticide residues, are plainly of the highest importance.

When people are cynical about the UN, it is worth drawing their attention to the positive achievements. Here are a few: 800 million men, women and children freed from malaria; 150 million in 61 countries vaccinated against tuberculosis; 350 million examined and where necessary treated for yaws and other tropical diseases; 2 million treated for leprosy; 2,700,000 acres of land irrigated in Pakistan, research into locust controls, rice production doubled in Egypt, Sudan, Yugoslavia; elementary and advanced training for technicians, factory workers, managers, nurses, educators and others brought into the most needy countries; North and South, East and West cooperating in all this. Over 300 multilateral agreements achieved through the UN—without counting the specialized agencies. Fifty disputes arbitrated by the World Court.

I am going to take the liberty of quoting at length from a remarkable meditation by Robert Muller, Secretary of the Economic and Social Council, in which that great international Civil Servant, after thirty years of world service, expresses in a challenging form his articles of faith in the UN:

The UN has

—helped one billion people gain national independence with a minimum of bloodshed, thus completing the historical movement started 200 years ago by the Declaration of Independence;

—helped the emergence of the poorer countries into the modern age, providing a safety lid for the explosive feelings of our less fortunate brethren at the injustices which prevail in the world;

—provided a talking place and a meeting ground during the worst periods of the cold war;

125

—provided for the first time in history a code of ethics for the relations between the most powerful institutions on Earth: armed nations;

—prevented, by its mere existence, even more national political and military adventures;

—provided a covering lid for hot conflicts, a standstill for fighting, a separation of belligerents and a talking ground between them;

—fared better with any conflict brought before it than unilateral, forceful attempts at settlement;

—been a moral force for progress toward political maturity, defusion of tensions, better understanding and reason around the world, proving that talking and listening are the beginning of wisdom and peace in human relations;

—been a platform for the expression and defense of all basic human aspirations, including those of liberty, equality and fraternity proclaimed by the American and French revolutions on the eve of the modern age;

—enhanced immensely a planetary acceptance of the racial equality of all human beings;

—warned mankind of its global limits and environmental constraints;

—progressively developed into a functional system of world order, covering with its large number of specialised agencies, programmes, centres, organs and units almost every field of human concern.

The UN is

—the first universal, global instrument mankind has ever had;

—the best chance of governments and nations to remain the permanent political and administrative units of planet Earth, provided they use and make the UN work to the satisfaction of the peoples;

—the place where new ethical values for nations and mankind are evolving;

—the best chance to keep within bounds new forms of transnational power and to develop codes of conduct for them;

—the central, permanent meeting ground of all human aspirations in which will be moulded a peaceful, just, safe and happy future for the human race;

—a treasure-house of world information;

—an incipient brain of the human species, registering global dangers and tendencies, keeping world conditions and phenomena under constant review, and fostering a better knowledge of our planet's resources and constraints;

—an incipient nervous system of mankind, relaying global findings and warnings to governments, local collectivities and the peoples;

—an incipient conscience and heart of humanity, which speaks for what is good and against what is bad for humans; which advocates and fosters understanding, cooperation and humanitarian help instead of division, struggle and indifference among nations;

—an observatory into the future, since most problems facing mankind will derive from the expansion of the human species, and its massive transformation of the physical and living conditions of our planet;

—(an international mechanism) here at the precise moment when humanity is becoming one global, complex, interdependent unit in so many respects. This will be its greatest historical chance of success and usefulness to mankind.

The UN should

—never be bypassed by any nation or group of nations as humanity's peacekeeping force;

—be used faithfully, in accordance with the Charter and the pledge of compliance by each member government, for the settlement of conflicts and the maintenance and strengthening of world peace;

—be further strengthened and perfected as a warning tower for global trends and menaces;

—be further developed as the planet's central statistical office and data bank;

—be strengthened regionally bringing each continent to bear its full contribution and role in the total world order;

—never be bypassed as the forum for the consideration of any problems which are of a world-wide nature and of concern to all humans;

—see its links with the world scientific and academic community strengthened, since much of our planet's future will be shaped by new advances in science, technology and knowledge. The creation of the United Nations University constitutes, in this respect, a major historical step forward in world co-operation and human evolution.

Governments should

—respect, support, strengthen and constantly improve their first planetary instrument for world peace, justice, progress, diagnosis, cooperation, forecasting and management; fulfill faithfully their obligations toward the Charter, a fact which alone would bring about peace, order and understanding in the world.

—implement the recommendations of the UN, above all by putting an end to the obsolete, insane and wasteful armaments race;

—teach our children and youth about the global age we are entering and the global intergovernmental instruments which have been created to help cope with it;

—enlist the impatience, idealism and energy of youth in building a better world, free of war, want, hatred and injustice;

—join their efforts in an unprecedented way to better explore, utilise and conserve the resources of our planet;

—promote a real revolution in world cooperation for the common benefit of the whole human race;

—better inform and educate the people about the work and efforts of the UN and its specialised agencies, thereby giving them confidence that something is being done about the problems which confront mankind on a global scale;

—enlist the support and better understanding of parliamentarians for world cooperation which is of direct interest and consequence to their electorates;

—turn their eyes away from the past and direct them to the future;

—plan for the arrival of several billion more people on this planet;

—extend their vision and concern to the whole planet, to all peoples and to all future generations instead of seeing, defending and often promoting narrow, immediate and transient national interests.

The people should

—have faith in the future and give a chance to the most noble attempt at world peace and cooperation ever undertaken on a universal basis;

—take an interest in the UN, its peacekeeping and peacemaking activities, its specialised agencies, its organs, its information, its studies, its meetings, its recommendations, its publications, its programmes, its world conferences;

—support, join or create volunteer groups or associations for the UN in order to be better informed about the efforts of *their* UN, and discuss the issues before it;

—request that children be educated about the world's global problems which affect every citizen, and about existing global intergovernmental efforts and instruments;

—demand from the news media more information about global problems and global efforts for peace, justice and a better world;

—request their political representatives to take a greater interest in world cooperation and developments which have become affairs of concern to all peoples;

—inform themselves of the efforts of the more than 5,000 international non-governmental organizations which in a vast number of professional, humanitarian and scientific fields foster international cooperation, friendship and common concerns;

—act and behave in greater cognizance of the fact that, in a world of several billion people, peace, progress, justice, understanding and the quality of life are essentially the sum total of the peace, progress, justice, understanding and quality of life of all individuals.

On the last day of his life Franklin Delano Roosevelt wrote these words for a speech he intended to deliver at the San Francisco Conference which launched the United Nations:

The work, my friends, is peace: more than an end of this war—an end to the beginning of all wars. I ask you to keep up your faith. The only limit to our realization of tomorrow will be our doubts of today. Let us move forward with a strong and active faith.

Index

134

We hope you enjoy this book. Please return or renew it by the due date.

You can renew it at www.norfolk.gov.uk/libraries or by using our free library app.

Otherwise you can phone 0344 800 8020 - please have your library card and PIN ready.

You can sign up for email reminders too.

Alex Delaware Novels

Serpentine (2021)	*Therapy* (2004)
The Museum of Desire (2020)	*A Cold Heart* (2003)
The Wedding Guest (2019)	*The Murder Book* (2002)
Night Moves (2018)	*Flesh and Blood* (2001)
Heartbreak Hotel (2017)	*Dr. Death* (2000)
Breakdown (2016)	*Monster* (1999)
Motive (2015)	*Survival of the Fittest* (1997)
Killer (2014)	*The Clinic* (1997)
Guilt (2013)	*The Web* (1996)
Victims (2012)	*Self-Defense* (1995)
Mystery (2011)	*Bad Love* (1994)
Deception (2010)	*Devil's Waltz* (1993)
Evidence (2009)	*Private Eyes* (1992)
Bones (2008)	*Time Bomb* (1990)
Compulsion (2008)	*Silent Partner* (1989)
Obsession (2007)	*Over the Edge* (1987)
Gone (2006)	*Blood Test* (1986)
Rage (2005)	*When the Bough Breaks* (1985)

BY JONATHAN KELLERMAN AND JESSE KELLERMAN

The Burning (2021)	*Crime Scene* (2017)
Half Moon Bay (2020)	*The Golem of Paris* (2015)
A Measure of Darkness (2018)	*The Golem of Hollywood* (2014)

OTHER NOVELS

The Murderer's Daughter (2015)	*Double Homicide* (with
True Detectives (2009)	Faye Kellerman, 2004)
Capital Crimes (with Faye	*The Conspiracy Club* (2003)
Kellerman, 2006)	*Billy Straight* (1998)
Twisted (2004)	*The Butcher's Theater* (1988)

GRAPHIC NOVELS

Silent Partner (2012)
The Web (2012)

NONFICTION

With Strings Attached: The Art and	*Helping the Fearful Child* (1981)
Beauty of Vintage Guitars (2008)	*Psychological Aspects of*
Savage Spawn: Reflections on Violent	*Childhood Cancer* (1980)
Children (1999)	

FOR CHILDREN, WRITTEN AND ILLUSTRATED

Jonathan Kellerman's ABC of Weird Creatures (1995)
Daddy, Daddy, Can You Touch the Sky? (1994)